Beyond Burnout: A New Zealand Guide

How To Spot It, Stop It And Stamp It Out

Suzi McAlpine

16pt

Copyright Page from the Original Book

RANDOM HOUSE

UK | USA | Canada | Ireland | Australia
India | New Zealand | South Africa | China

Random House is an imprint of the Penguin Random House group of companies, whose addresses can be found at global.penguinrandomhouse.com.

First published by Penguin Random House New Zealand, 2021

10 9 8 7 6 5 4 3 2 1

Text © Suzi McAlpine, 2021

The moral right of the author has been asserted.

All rights reserved. Without limiting the rights under copyright reserved above, no part of this publication may be reproduced, stored in or introduced into a retrieval system, or transmitted, in any form or by any means (electronic, mechanical, photocopying, recording or otherwise), without the prior written permission of both the copyright owner and the above publisher of this book.

Design by Cat Taylor © Penguin Random House New Zealand
Illustrations by Cat Taylor, except: adjusted stock imagery from Getty Images by ourlifelooklikeballoon (p. 31), Zdenek Sasek (p. 77), Shendart (p. 106), S-S-S (p. 110); and from Creative Market by Good Stuff No Nonsense (p. 100).
Cover photograph by Eshma via iStock
Prepress by Image Centre Group
Printed and bound in Australia by Griffin Press, an Accredited ISO AS/NZS 14001 Environmental Management Systems Printer

A catalogue record for this book is available from the National Library of New Zealand.

penguin.co.nz

TABLE OF CONTENTS

FOREWORD	ii
PREFACE	vi
INTRODUCTION	xi
CHAPTER 1: THE COST OF BURNOUT	1
CHAPTER 2: MYTHS OF BURNOUT	18
CHAPTER 3: WHAT IS BURNOUT?	46
CHAPTER 4: WHO IS MOST AT RISK OF BURNOUT?	66
CHAPTER 5: WHAT CAUSES BURNOUT?	94
CHAPTER 6: WHAT WE CAN DO TO ADDRESS BURNOUT	132
CHAPTER 7: RECOGNISE	149
CHAPTER 8: DESTIGMATISE	185
CHAPTER 9: SOCIALISE	219
CHAPTER 10: ORGANISE	256
CHAPTER 11: SO YOU THINK YOU MIGHT HAVE BURNOUT – NOW WHAT?	295
CHAPTER 12: I'M LEADING SOMEONE WHO I SUSPECT MIGHT BE BURNED OUT – NOW WHAT?	322
BEYOND BURNOUT – SUMMING IT ALL UP	337
APPENDIX A: THE COGO WORKPLACE WELLBEING SURVEY 2020	350
APPENDIX B: THE STAGES OF BURNOUT	357
APPENDIX C: STRESS IDENTIFICATION DIARY	362
APPENDIX D: MONTHLY ONE-ON-ONES	367
APPENDIX E: IDENTIFYING STRENGTHS AND ENCOURAGING PEOPLE TO WORK FROM THEM	373
APPENDIX F: THE TIME MANAGEMENT MATRIX	377
APPENDIX G: SOME USEFUL COACHING QUESTIONS FOR LEADERS	385

APPENDIX H: HOW TO IMPROVE YOUR EMOTIONAL INTELLIGENCE 388
APPENDIX I: DELEGATION MODEL 392
APPENDIX J: A PRACTICAL EXERCISE FOR BUILDING A COLLECTIVE VISION AND TRUST WITH YOUR TEAM 399
APPENDIX K: THE WHEEL OF LIFE 407
APPENDIX L: FURTHER RESOURCES 413
REFERENCES 417
ACKNOWLEDGEMENTS 442
ABOUT THE AUTHOR 448
PRAISE FOR BEYOND BURNOUT 450
Index 455

For Dad, who always told me to stop and smell the roses

FOREWORD

My mental health journey has been ongoing for many years and during that time I have discovered that the most important aspect when we talk about it is the ability to change the dialogue and to normalise discussion of mental health. I have found that often, mental health is seen as a topic that is not to be mentioned in polite company or in our organisations. I have spent much of my time over these many years bringing the topic of mental health into the light, not only by talking about my own journey, but hopefully, by also making it easier for others to talk about theirs.

The topic of burnout is, I believe, a really good way to get through to people about mental health in a normalised manner—encouraging them to consider what is going on both in their lives and the lives of others. From a business perspective, burnout is now becoming a common issue that organisations and managers need to think about in order to ensure that they can assist with their people's wellbeing and mental health.

When it's extreme, burnout means you cannot work anymore. This can lead to extended periods away from the workforce. But unfortunately, there are also many people who are working in a suboptimal manner because of the effects of burnout. This is much more difficult to see and then be able to intervene.

We need to focus on making earlier interventions. We need to make sure that we put a fence around the top of the cliff—and in the long run, get to the point the ambulance at the bottom is no longer required. That change, while simple to say, is much harder in practice to do. So when I come across others like Suzi, who have found ways to help this happen, I want to take the time to engage, as this change is so important to me.

What I really liked about this book is the many practical and pragmatic tips that will increase our businesses' and managers' ability to put simple actions into place that will help their people avoid burnout in the workplace. As well as considering burnout from a business perspective and what leaders can do, this book also offers the same practical advice to individuals themselves, again in a simple and understandable manner.

In what is an increasingly complex world, there is a clear need to raise awareness of the importance of mental health. This includes building a greater understanding of burnout. It also means learning and applying the tips and techniques that the business, the manager or you can use to make sure that burnout in the workplace can effectively be avoided. This book provides the tools to help people to build that fence at the top of the cliff and this is what I am so excited about. It is work like this that increases my faith that mental health can become an everyday topic of conversation with no stigma attached.

So, I would like to congratulate Suzi on her important focus on burnout in the workplace and I know that by encouraging people to talk about this topic, she is greatly assisting my drive to normalise the discussion of mental health. If we can start by acknowledging burnout as a common issue for many individuals, then it is the first step in providing a happier, healthier workplace.

Sir John Kirwan
November 2020

PREFACE

This was not the book I intended to write. My first book idea was on a very different topic, relating to leadership. It led me to spend a truckload of time and money researching and writing, culminating in a research trip to New York and the American Midwest to interview several world experts on said leadership topic.

The whole trip was a train wreck.

In the weeks and months leading up to it, I had felt a gnawing sense that although this was a great idea for a book that most definitely needed to be written, I might not be the right person to write it. But I pushed my intuition down and ploughed on. I was aware of the time and energy I'd already invested. Sunk costs can be applied to book writing as much as anything else, as it happens.

Although I think I knew deep down that this was not my story, nor the right book for me to write, as it was outside my area of expertise, I consciously had this epiphany in a hotel room in New York. I had just stepped out of the shower—hair dripping—and was sitting on the end of my bed in a hotel bathrobe, 10,000 miles away from my home in New Zealand. In that moment, I realised I had let my head and some innate desire to prove myself overtake what I knew to be true. I had not listened to or trusted my inner voice.

It was not an enjoyable epiphany. I limped home with a humiliating hole in my wallet, my ego and my book-writing vision.

But this failure, this 'book topic misstep', was actually an important detour in the right direction that ultimately led me here—and to writing this book. And *this* is most definitely the book that was mine to write. I have experienced burnout myself. And throughout my career in executive search and latterly as an executive coach, I've had a front row seat to many executives' experiences of burnout.

The more I researched burnout, the more I saw what a growing problem it's becoming—across industries, professions and organisational hierarchies. And the more steps I took on this burnout book journey, the more people wanted to tell me their stories of burnout, too. I realised that it's far more widespread than we would like to think. As I explored further, I soon began to come to grips with the fact that leaders and organisations can (and do) play a significant role in whether or not their employees experience burnout.

Writing this book has been personally confronting at times. I'd like to say that burnout is something I suffered from once, learnt from, then put to bed. But looking back, I see that my experience has been something of a repetitive dance with burnout. I can think of at least two times in my career when I was, in hindsight, in the quagmire that is burnout, even if I didn't recognise it as that at the time.

There are lots of books about burnout, but almost all of them are geared exclusively towards the person suffering from it. They cover what to do to avoid it, what to do if you're suffering from it, and how to recover from it. At first, this annoyed the heck out of me, and I wasn't sure why. Yet the more I looked into this topic, the more I began to realise why I found this frustrating.

Leaders and organisations are necessarily at the crux of any discussion of burnout. For too long, we've placed far too much onus on the individual who is suffering burnout for both its avoidance and its remedy—and not enough on the organisations and leadership practices which have, in many cases, caused it in the first place.

On top of this, I quickly began to realise that most organisations and leaders don't actually have the necessary knowledge and tools to tackle burnout in the workplace. Increasingly, we're coming to understand the importance of mental wellbeing at work, but we're still not exactly sure *how* to go about tackling it.

It's time that we change the conversation around burnout (and, perhaps by default, mental wellbeing in the workplace more generally). I want to bring a leadership lens to burnout, as well as looking at how it affects individuals. After all, leaders are people—and all people, to an extent, can be leaders. Not only that, but this is my world. Leadership is what I know well.

Finally, I want to bring a uniquely Antipodean lens to workplace stress and burnout. There's a plethora of research and books written on burnout overseas, but very little has been done from a Kiwi or Aussie viewpoint. I was curious about this. What might be different? What might be the same?

So although I have been saying that I am writing a book for more years than I care to admit, what you are holding now in your hands has been about four years in the making. I've been on the front line, and my thinking has been able to evolve and deepen over time. While it began in that hotel room, with my hair dripping wet, this book came via the realisation that my own burnout journey, and those I have witnessed, places me in a unique position to share what can be done to spot it, stop it and stamp it out.

INTRODUCTION

It was a Tuesday morning in late 2008, but it is seared into my memory as if it happened yesterday.

From the outside, it looked like I had it all. My life was awash with professional pinnacles and shiny badges of success. I was in my mid-thirties, a senior executive in the New Zealand division of the world's largest HR consulting and executive-search firm. I'd recently received a promotion and had come back from parental leave early, to lead our practice through the global financial crisis (GFC). I had a growing family of three children—my youngest daughter was just shy of six months old—and my husband was busy with his first CEO role.

My life was full to the brim—overflowing, even. I was one of those 'go-get 'em', high-achieving professional women. My friends used to call me Super Suzi. I wore that badge with honour, even if it did weigh me down a little.

Every morning, I'd jumble the kids into the back of the car, gulping down a piece of cold toast, with baby spittle on my crisp navy suit as I careened out of the driveway. I'd hurl the kids out of the car doors at their respective schools and day cares, and tear into Auckland's CBD for a meeting with some bigwig CEO from some bigwig corporate organisation about leading the search to find some other bigwig executive.

On this particular Tuesday morning, my then seven-year-old son Nicholas clambered out of the back seat of the car as we pulled up outside his school. As he did, he turned to me, hesitated and asked, voice trembling, 'Mummy ... can I please have a hug?'

This was a big deal. Nicholas was not a physically affectionate kid, so for him to reach out and proactively ask for a hug was unusual. He'd been struggling a little at school, and his teacher had told us he had been crying a lot when he got something wrong. It was another thing on my list of things to sort out.

However, in that moment, his trembling words didn't compute with me. I glanced over at him, then looked over his shoulder, my mind racing anxiously through the presentation I had to give in 30 minutes. Then I shoved him and his little backpack onto the pavement and replied in a clipped, rushed, stressed-out tone, 'No! I don't have time.'

I slammed the door in his dear little face and drove off, leaving him standing alone on the footpath.

To this day, the look in my son's eyes in the rear-view mirror haunts me.

A few minutes later, I pulled over to the side of the road—sobbing so hard I could no longer see to navigate my way through rush-hour traffic. The numbness that had surrounded me like a thick blanket of sense-dulling fog just minutes earlier had evaporated. It was replaced by the searing, heart-wrenching realisation of what I had just done.

'What just happened?' I sobbed. '*Who am I!?* Why don't I even have the headspace to hug my wee man?' Berating myself, despairing puddles of tears mixed with the baby vomit on my navy suit.

I'm usually a very warm and affectionate person. That's how I'm often described by people who meet me. But something was very wrong here. I had become so numb and emotionally distant that I couldn't even connect with one of the most important people in my life when he needed me.

Yet, as agonising as this moment was, I now know it was the wakeup call I needed. Someone had thrown a bucket of icy water in my face that Tuesday morning. That moment in the car, on the side of the road, was the moment when I realised things weren't as rosy on the inside as they seemed from the outside.

Although up until then my job had afforded me significant insights into the experiences of many burned-out senior executives (and it still does), this was the first time I'd really come up-close and personal with this thing called burnout. With hindsight, I now know I was in the thick of it. I was exhibiting one of the key signs of burnout—emotional distance and depersonalisation. And it wasn't just showing up in my relationship with my boy. My interactions with friends and loved ones were mechanical and distracted. At work, my usual enthusiasm and focus on possibilities had evaporated, replaced by robotic and distant leadership. I had started to feel like a failure.

And so began my own burnout journey, one which has taught me to better recognise the signs of burnout in myself and take steps to climb out of its debilitating quicksand. It has also helped me to see burnout more clearly in the people I have led—and to help them, too. These days, as a leadership coach, the journey continues. When I burned out, I never suspected I was joining a long list of business leaders who had suffered from the same thing.

Nor did I imagine that, eventually, my burnout journey would lead me to write this book.

WHY YOU SHOULD READ THIS BOOK

This book is not just for stressed-out, burned-out executives—although it will be super handy if that *is* you. It's for those of you who know there must be ways to achieve productivity and effectiveness, and execute strategy successfully—but not by burning out people (including yourself) in the process. You might be someone who has experienced or is experiencing burnout. You might be leading someone who you suspect is experiencing burnout, or have a loved one suffering from it. It's my hope that you are—at whatever level within your organisation—a leader who wants to create teams or organisations where people, as well as profits, thrive.

Burnout is not a new phenomenon, but it's a growing one. It's a big problem in our workplaces, regardless of which industry or profession you're in or where you sit on the organisational ladder. And it's a problem that's getting bigger by the year. A 2018 Gallup study of nearly 7500 full-time employees internationally found that 23 per cent reported feeling burned out at work *very often or always,* while an additional 44 per cent reported feeling burned out sometimes. That translates to about two-thirds of full-time workers experiencing burnout on the job. And it's estimated that 1 million workers are absent every day globally due to stress, causing losses for larger companies in excess of US$3.5 million per company, per year.

Covid-19 has also had an impact. A survey by Blind, an anonymous workplace community app, of over 6000 employees, reported an increase in burnout after Covid-19 emerged. In February 2020, 61 per cent of professionals considered that they were burned out. That number rose to 73 per cent between April and May 2020, when the Covid-19 pandemic was really taking hold.

Although there are plenty of books on burnout, most of them are targeted solely towards the person who's suffering from it. This book is different. It tackles the root causes of burnout, and it helps leaders, organisations *and* individuals create the conditions that help organisations *and people* thrive, not burn out. It also provides practical tools that individuals, leaders and organisations can use to combat burnout and the enormous costs it creates.

HERE'S WHAT YOU'LL LEARN

You'll learn about the significant costs of burnout, to both individuals and companies. Then, we'll shatter some common burnout myths.

We'll take a closer look at what burnout is—and what it isn't. We'll ask questions like:
- What exactly is burnout?
- What's the difference between 'just' being stressed and being burned out?

And we'll outline why stress itself isn't the problem.

*

You might also be wondering who is most likely to suffer from burnout and who is more likely to be immune, so we will take a look at who is most at risk. Spoiler alert: no one is immune—anyone can suffer from burnout. That said, there are certain professions, industries and personality types who are more at risk than others.

Second spoiler alert: high performers often fall into that category.

Understanding the most significant causes of burnout is critical if you want to prevent it. Yes, there's the obvious issue of overwork. But there are also some other causes that you might be surprised to discover. We'll explore what they are.

Knowing all these things is vital in the fight against burnout. But what can actually be done to prevent and tackle this 'bigger than *Ben Hur*' problem that's seeping into the psyche of many organisations? The good news is that there are practical steps individuals, leaders and organisations can take.

Without a doubt, leadership plays a crucial role in burnout prevention—but this isn't reserved for traditional leaders only. Regardless of your level in an organisation, everyone can play a role in protecting our organisations, our teams and ourselves from burnout. We're going to cover the role that leadership plays in burnout prevention—and include a 'how to' guide at the end of each of the latter chapters for leaders, organisations and individuals alike.

In those later chapters, we will look at the four '-ises' I have coined—Recognise, Destigmatise, Socialise and Organise. These strategies are key to tackling burnout. I'll explain each concept in more detail and show you practical steps for how you can adopt them, whether it's from an individual, leadership or organisational perspective.

Here's the rub: burnout doesn't cause issues solely for the person experiencing it. It's also hindering organisational performance and costing billions in lost revenue, productivity and engagement. It's wreaking havoc on people's personal lives—on families and loved ones—as well as on people's health and their experience of professional life. And it's preventing our businesses from being the places they have the potential to be.

It's time we changed that. This book will show you how.

CHAPTER 1

THE COST OF BURNOUT

'The burnout of employees is a symptom of bigger problems within each organisation. It has a negative effect on nearly every aspect of a business. From excessive tardiness and absenteeism to lack of employee engagement, burnout is sneaky and damaging over time.'
Writer and marketer Eve Davies-Greenwald

When I experienced burnout all those years ago, the shame and embarrassment I felt about being exhausted and overwhelmed meant that I shared my experiences with only a handful of people. This was in part because I thought I was alone in feeling this overwhelmed. At the very least, feeling burned out was not something many people around me were publicly admitting to experiencing. Open and frank conversations about burnout aren't usually high on the list for water-cooler conversations or business meetings in many workplaces!

But I was wrong about being alone. One of the biggest epiphanies I've had in writing and researching this book is that burnout is far more common than I'd originally thought. What's more, its prevalence in our organisations is growing—along with the associated costs.

If you think the experience of burnout is relegated to only a small, unfortunate few—and that the costs of burnout are relatively insignificant—you might want to pay close attention to this chapter. In it, I show you how burnout is on the rise. I outline some startling costs associated with burnout that are affecting our organisations and societies alike. And I make a case for us to start paying closer attention to people's mental wellbeing in the workplace—in particular, the effects of high stress and burnout.

HOW PREVALENT IS BURNOUT, REALLY?

Burnout is not a new phenomenon. It's been around, in one shape or another, for almost as long as humans have been working. Although the term 'burnout' was officially coined by German-born American psychologist Herbert Freudenberger in 1974, there are descriptions of burnout found in many historical records—across different times and in different cultures. According to some researchers, reports of feelings that we would associate with burnout can be found from the Old Testament to Shakespeare's writings!

But one thing's for sure: it's a malaise of increasing prevalence in the twenty-first century. Take the findings from the US General Social Survey of 2016 as an example. Tracking the attitudes and behaviours of American society since 1972, this survey found that, in 2016, 50 per cent of respondents were consistently exhausted because of work, compared with just 18 per cent two decades ago.

More people suffer from burnout than you might think. According to a 2019 report by American analytics and advisory company, Gallup, *Employee Burnout: Causes and Cures,* 76 per cent of employees experience burnout on the job at least sometimes, and 28 per cent say they are burned out 'very often' or 'always' at work. And in Deloitte's 2015 external marketplace survey of 1000 full-time US professionals, which explored the drivers and impact of employee burnout, 77 per cent of respondents said that they had experienced employee burnout at their current job, with more than half citing more than one occurrence.

These startling statistics are what we need to sit up and take notice of, especially from a leadership perspective.

Anyone can suffer from burnout, but, as I mentioned above, the rates are higher in certain professions. Those which are passion-driven and caregiving-centred (such as the medical, front-line services, social work, legal and teaching professions) are some of the most susceptible to burnout.

Take surgeons, for example. When I gave a keynote speech at the Royal Australasian College of Surgeons conference in Bangkok in 2019, I told the audience that the burnout rate in their profession is more than 50 per cent. Many surgeons nodded (exhaustedly), and the conversations I had with delegates afterwards backed up this startling figure.

We all have the occasional day when we feel like we'd rather pull up the covers and stay in bed, or when we drag our feet to work because we're just not 'feeling it'. But tiredness and emotional drain related to work is occurring in our workplaces far more than many realise. In fact, if you think of just one of your co-workers, one or the other of you is likely to be feeling this way at any given time.

A 2020 Workplace Wellbeing Survey conducted by research agency Cogo made some concerning revelations regarding burnout in Australasia. Cogo surveyed more than 1500 people across the New Zealand and Australian workforces, and more than half of the respondents (61 per cent) showed signs of **exhaustion,** a key indicator of burnout. This meant that well over half answered 'every day' or 'a few times a week' to the question 'How often do you feel tired when you get up in the morning and have to face another day on the job?' and/or 'How often do you feel emotionally drained from your work?'.

What's also concerning is how *often* people are experiencing these main symptoms of burnout: in many cases, every day or at least a few times a week.

The Cogo study found that:
- 30 per cent of respondents showed signs of **isolation** (answering 'every day' or 'a few times a week' to 'How often do you feel misunderstood or unappreciated by your co-workers?')
- 32 per cent of respondents showed signs of **depersonalisation** (answering 'every day' or 'a few times a week' to 'How often do you feel that you are harder and less sympathetic with people at work than perhaps they deserve?' and/or 'How often are you easily irritated

by small problems or by your co-workers?')
- 57 per cent of respondents showed signs of a **lack of engagement** (answering 'every day' or 'a few times a week' to 'How often do you think about leaving your current place of work?' and/or agreeing that '...recently you have become less enthusiastic about your work')
- 11 per cent of respondents showed signs of **low professional efficacy** (answering 'not very confident' or 'not at all confident' to 'How confident are you that you are effective at getting things done at work?' and/or 'How confident are you that you can effectively solve problems that crop up in your work?').

Half of respondents showed one or both of the following signs of **cynicism:**
- 19 per cent felt that they 'make a valuable contribution to the business or organisation' just 'a few times a month' or less, and
- two-thirds (66 per cent) said that 'work politics or bureaucracy get in

the way of [their] ability to do a good job' more than once a week.

You can read more about this study in Appendix A.

Despite many organisations thinking they are making efforts to address stress in the workplace, it seems we're missing the mark a lot of the time when it comes to developing wellbeing programmes that employees find valuable. Cogo's research indicates we're falling short in New Zealand and Australia when it comes to how we're running wellbeing programmes in our workplaces:

- 81 per cent of respondents to the 2020 survey reported that their workplace offers at least one programme or service to support mental or physical wellbeing in the workplace. But—and this is the concerning part—only 40 per cent of respondents 'strongly agree' or 'agree' that, overall, their workplace does a good job at supporting mental and physical wellbeing.
- We're seeing a low uptake of the programmes and services offered by workplaces, too. These had been

accessed by less than half of those to which they had been offered (except healthy food and/or drinks, which were accessed by 74 per cent of survey respondents who had been offered them). This suggests that there are issues with how employees are engaging with these services and programmes or with how they're targeted and/or communicated.

Not to put a further downer on things, but it would seem that we're also becoming more tired and lonely at work than ever before. According to the US General Social Survey of 2016, people are twice as likely to report that they're always exhausted compared with roughly 20 years ago. Close to 50 per cent of people said that they were often or always exhausted due to work—a 32 per cent increase from two decades earlier! This is not how it should be.

Researchers Emma Seppälä and Marissa King warn us in their *Harvard Business Review* article 'Burnout at Work Isn't Just About Exhaustion. It's Also About Loneliness', 'This is a shockingly high statistic. What's more, there is a significant correlation between feeling lonely and work exhaustion: the more people are exhausted, the lonelier they feel.' Given loneliness is one of the main causes of burnout, all in all that's a worrying interdependent and symbiotic relationship.

The global Covid-19 pandemic is adding extra stress for many people. Many of the causes of burnout which we delve into later in the book are made worse by the conditions in the unprecedented Covid-19-fuelled climate. Unsurprisingly, early research indications are that Covid-19 is an added stressor for employees and employers alike—unlikely to be news to anybody!

But many of the biggest contributors to burnout, for example overwork, are more constant and inbuilt in today's work environments, and it's these factors that are playing a bigger role in burnout. It's important we don't fall prey to automatically blaming Covid-19 for all our burnout woes. (The Cogo Workplace Wellbeing Survey had some interesting results on this. Those citing Covid-19 as a source of stress at work showed slightly higher levels of exhaustion—69 per cent versus the total sample average of 61 per cent.) That said, Covid has had nowhere near as big an impact on exhaustion as more common sources of stress such as bullying and harassment, discrimination or having an unrealistically high workload.

One thing from the research is clear: more people are suffering from burnout than ever before. And the costs associated with burnout are growing alongside this rise. For this reason alone, this book is one to read—whether you're a senior manager or an individual contributor in your workplace.

We can all play a role in reversing these statistics.

THE COST OF BURNOUT TO ORGANISATIONS

The costs of burnout for the people experiencing it are obvious. But the costs of burnout are significant to organisations too. Before we delve into these further, it's worth pausing for a moment to step back and examine just how important people are to an organisation and the economy.

People are a critical factor in an organisation's success, but many CEOs don't appreciate their significance. An economic analysis commissioned by management consultancy Korn Ferry found that human capital represents a potential value of US$1.2 *quadrillion* for the global economy—more than twice the value of tangible assets such as technology and real estate. Despite this, the survey uncovered some pretty worrying mental models among CEOs. A total of 67 per cent of CEOs believed that technology will create greater value in the future than human capital will. Further to that, 63 per cent of CEOs perceive that technology will become their firm's greatest source of future competitive advantage.

But the economic reality differs sharply. It's human capital, *not* physical capital, which creates the greatest value for organisations. As the authors of the study pointed out, 'CEOs have a significant blind spot in the way they perceive people, tending to undervalue human capital ... Although organisations obsess over technology and its promise, people hold huge, measurable value. And they can't be neglected in the future of work.'

This is an important backdrop when we consider the costs of burnout in our organisations and in our society through a purely economic lens. But the costs of burnout extend way beyond just simple economics; they include real damage to people's health and wellbeing.

The impact of burnout on people's professional and personal lives, their health and wellbeing—and even their careers—is well documented. But burnout also wreaks havoc on an organisation's performance. Lost productivity, absenteeism, presenteeism and poor employee engagement are just a few key organisational-health measurements that are negatively impacted by burnout. And for those of you who are financially inclined, it's also not great for the bottom line either!

According to the O.C. Tanner 2020 Global Culture Report, burnout is the cause of:

- a 220 per cent decrease in the probability of highly engaged employees
- a 210 per cent decrease in the odds an employee will be a promoter of the organisation
- a 247 per cent decrease in the probability of great work happening
- half of annual employee turnover
- a 23 per cent increase in the likelihood of an employee visiting the emergency room
- an increased risk of Type 2 diabetes, coronary heart disease, gastrointestinal issues and high cholesterol
- $190 billion USD in healthcare spending, plus 120,000 deaths per year.

These statistics, which are echoed in other studies, are enough to give any CEO a headache.

Burnout is like rocket fuel for absenteeism. The Cogo Workplace Wellbeing Survey showed that 34 per cent of all respondents had taken leave in the past year because of stress. But when Cogo looked at those who were demonstrating the key signs of burnout, outlined below, the numbers skyrocketed.

- 44 per cent of respondents showing signs of **exhaustion** had taken leave in the past year because of stress, compared with just 19 per cent of those who didn't show signs of exhaustion. That means those showing signs of exhaustion were 2.4 times more likely to have taken leave in the past year because of stress.
- 55 per cent of those showing signs of **isolation** had taken leave in the past year because of stress, compared with just 25 per cent of those who didn't show signs of isolation. That means those showing signs of isolation were 2.2 times more likely to have taken leave in the past year because of stress.
- 52 per cent of respondents showing signs of **depersonalisation** had taken leave in the past year because of stress, compared with just 26 per cent of those who didn't show signs of depersonalisation, making them twice as likely to have

taken leave in the past year because of stress.

If I were a CEO or senior executive, these figures would be cause for concern.

But it's not just CEOs who should be worried by the burnout research; many HR professionals are seeing up close the effects of burnout too. A US survey conducted by Kronos Incorporated and Future Workplace found that 95 per cent of human resource leaders admit employee burnout is sabotaging workforce retention.

Consider also the fact that companies without systems to support the wellbeing of their employees have even higher turnover, lower productivity and higher healthcare costs, according to the American Psychological Association (APA).

The fact that the World Health Organization has reportedly predicted that burnout will become a global pandemic in ten years is a sobering indictment on where we're headed if we don't address burnout effectively. And soon.

If all of these facts are a bit, well, overwhelming—take heart. In the following chapters, we delve into burnout—its causes and symptoms and, perhaps most importantly, what we can all do to reverse this worrying trend.

CHAPTER 2
MYTHS OF BURNOUT

'For the great enemy of truth is very often not the lie—deliberate, contrived and dishonest—but the myth—persistent, persuasive, and unrealistic.'

John F. Kennedy

Although the word 'burnout' is a term everyone has heard of, it's still largely misunderstood. It has become part of our workplace vernacular, although the way we refer to it often adds to the misunderstanding of what it actually is. We often describe everyday stress as burnout when it is, in fact, not. 'Man, I'm so burned out after that week from hell!' we lament after a stressful week, not realising that true burnout is something altogether different and far more malevolent.

When an organisational phenomenon is misunderstood, it's a breeding ground for misconceptions. And the trouble with misconceptions—like the ones I outline in this chapter—is that they're often unconsciously held mental models. They're common opinion, but we assume they're fact. And because of this, they form our basis for making decisions.

Take, for example, commonly held misconceptions about the leadership practice of coaching. Many managers believe that coaching takes a lot of time and that it's something leaders need to do *on top of* leading, when in fact it's just an *approach* to leading. Not only that—a coaching conversation can take as little as three minutes. This misconception about the time it takes to coach others means that many leaders don't coach. And the reality is that if they did, it would actually *save* them time.

It's the same when we apply these sorts of misconceptions, myths and mental models to burnout. Making decisions about burnout from a place of unconscious assumptions (whether these have stemmed from an organisational or individual perspective) has harmful consequences—not only for the person experiencing burnout, but also for the organisation.

If we can begin to dispel some of the myths that circle burnout, we'll be far more effective in tackling it in our workplaces. So let's dive into some of the more common myths that I come across regularly.

MYTH ONE: BURNOUT IS ALL ABOUT THE PERSON, NOT THE WORKPLACE

One of the biggest and most insidious myths that surround burnout is that it is predominantly an individual's problem, not an organisational one.

I've alluded to this already, but we tend to put way too much onus on the individual to prevent, treat and recover from burnout in the workplace. The internet is awash with articles on burnout for the burned out. They offer an array of tips and tools, from yoga and mindfulness to resilience courses, prioritising and 'just saying no'. Although most of these strategies are useful, they're not enough. Nor is it merely the individual's responsibility to tackle burnout—because it's not an individual problem.

It's dangerous to look at burnout in a singular light, or to view the person suffering from burnout in isolation. In doing so, we forget that they're part of an ecosystem. And it's this ecosystem that is almost always at the root of the problem.

This is a bit like treating a sick fish when it's the water that's contaminated.

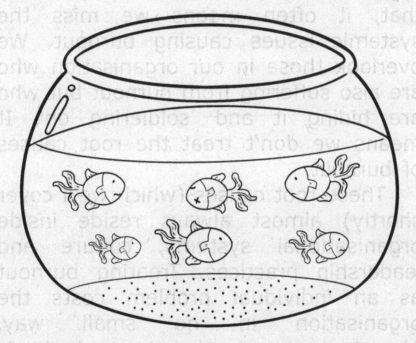

Sure, employees can take steps to remain resilient and productive at work. We can all do things which will help us address overwork, build social connection and prioritise our work. And if you're suffering from burnout, there are some very real and effective steps you can take to get back on track—we'll cover those later in the book.

But treating burnout predominantly as an individual problem is, in itself, problematic. For one, it can inadvertently assign blame to individuals for getting burned out, when it's the organisation that has caused it. Not only that, it often means we miss the systemic issues causing burnout. We overlook those in our organisation who are also suffering from burnout but who are hiding it and 'soldiering on'. It means we don't treat the root causes of burnout.

These root causes (which we'll cover shortly) almost always reside inside organisational systems, culture and leadership practices. Treating burnout as an individual problem costs the organisation in no small way. Absenteeism (and presenteeism), employee turnover, low engagement and ultimately an impact on profits are all products of burnout—as well as the effects on the person who's suffering from it.

> *'I feel my workplace offers certain resources around wellbeing in order to tick boxes. The workplace culture continues to be toxic ... but we can have three free counselling sessions if we want...'*
> Anonymous respondent, Cogo Workplace Wellbeing Survey 2020

There's another unintended damaging consequence of treating burnout like it's an individual problem, not an organisational one: it can be downright harmful to the employee who's suffering from burnout. By inadvertently seeming to *blame* the person who's suffering from burnout, while abdicating responsibility for doing much about it, this approach adds to the stigma of burnout. You see this played out a lot in the healthcare sector, for example.

> *'When I went to med school, everything was exciting. You hardly got anyone leaving med school. And then you do your clinical year and that's fine ... But then you start working in hospital settings and it's*

a kind of "sink or swim" situation. We had one guy leave before his final qualification ... A lot of the young ones coming through are just getting so stressed...'

Interview with Simon[1], medical professional who experienced burnout

Unless we start to view burnout in a more holistic, systemic way, we will continuously 'treat' sick fish—then put them back into the contaminated water, just to have them get sick again. In some cases, we even start to blame the fish for being weak, or somehow flawed, instead of taking a closer look at what's making them sick in the first place. Yep, that toxic water.

As social psychologist Christina Maslach, arguably the world's leading expert on burnout, said in a recent *Harvard Business Review* interview, 'When we just look at the person, what that means is, "Hey we've got to treat that person." "You can't work here because you're the problem." "We have

---

[1] The names of those interviewed for this book have been changed

to get rid of that person." Then, it becomes that person's problem, not the responsibility of the organisation that employs them.'

Which leads me to a second big myth about burnout...

MYTH TWO: PEOPLE WHO SUFFER FROM BURNOUT ARE MENTALLY WEAK, CAN'T HANDLE STRESS OR ARE POOR PERFORMERS

This is the other highly pervasive myth I come across. But take the chief executive of UK-based Lloyds Banking Group, António Horta-Osório as an example. This high-profile CEO, with an impressive track record of success, has had personal experience of burnout. In fact, it got so bad that he took leave from his role.

'I was very mindful that the bank was in a very weak position to face adversity. It was a problem that was going around my mind constantly, which led me to sleep

less and less. And the less and less sleep progressively led me to exhaustion, and then to not sleeping at all, which was a form of torture, so I had to address it and I did.'

Horta-Osório's story of burnout shows us how workplace stress can affect anyone—even those with stellar executive careers.

While there is this unconscious mindset that people who suffer from burnout are weak or poor performers, in many cases it's quite the opposite. In fact, it may be that the highest-performing, most dedicated and passionate workers are *most* at risk from burnout. A five-year study in the UK, released in 2017, found that the mental health of 20 per cent of the top-performing leaders of British businesses was affected by corporate burnout.

The fact is that many people who suffer from burnout have previously been high-performing and engaged employees. Burnout has even been described as 'overachiever syndrome'.

> *'I think actually the very high achieving people ... you really push yourselves and you expect enormous things from yourselves, and actually, you're your own worst critics.'*
>
> Simon, medical professional

Without blowing my own trumpet, take me as an example. I had always been seen as a high performer and had enjoyed regular promotions throughout my career. Although I had had my fair share of challenges and teeth-gnashing experiences in my professional life, I had always received positive performance reviews and had often been seen as 'key talent' in the companies I had worked for.

However, when I became burned out, not only did my self-confidence dive (I felt like I couldn't do the things I normally could, without Herculean effort) but my worries became a self-fulfilling prophecy. As I burned out, my efficiency and effectiveness dropped. I suddenly struggled to meet budgets. I couldn't make decisions, and I had trouble backing myself. For most of my professional life I had achieved; now I was most certainly not. This cut deep. It added bewilderment to my angst. I was working harder but going nowhere.

High performers may be more at risk of burnout for a number of reasons. Some of these are because of their personal tendencies and some of them result from their organisation's response to them as high performers.

Let's look first at the tendencies of high performers. An article in the *Harvard Business Review* in 2018 pointed to the common stereotype that high performers can struggle to maintain a healthy work–life balance. As Ryan O'Reilly, a high-performance coach, author and international speaker on performance and resilience, said in an article for *Silicon Republic,* 'High performers are more at risk of burnout because of their drive to do an excellent job all the time. Their personalities don't tend to lend themselves to do a half job on anything. This, coupled with the inability of the high performer to say "no", and adding more work onto their ever-increasing workloads, is why they are more likely to burn out. High performers are usually the ones who put in more hours and cancel personal engagements for work.'

But it's important not to put the blame squarely on the habits of high performers when it comes to the potential for burnout. Alongside these tendencies, let's take a look at the organisational response to high performers.

Unsurprisingly, high performers are often the ones assigned the most challenging projects. Not only that, but the breaks between these projects tend to be short, if they have one at all. Because they're deemed a top performer, others are constantly asking them for help. The expectations on high performers around mentoring others are also higher.

Next, consider overwork (a major cause of burnout) and the high performer. Who do leaders tend to give the new projects, high-priority tasks and the most important work they need to get done to? Yep, you guessed it: the most competent among the team. The adage 'If you want something done, give it to the busiest person' applies here. (I would add '...and the most high performing'.)

I saw this phenomenon first-hand when I was interviewing hundreds of high-performing senior executives in my role as an executive search consultant. Often, they would be given high-profile and critical organisational projects to lead on top of their 'business as usual' responsibilities because they were extremely competent.

However, many felt that they couldn't say no to these projects for fear that doing so may be career-limiting. In many cases, there was not sufficient negotiation on what responsibilities they could drop, even temporarily, in order to take on these projects. As a result, I often had many of these high-performing executives sitting in my office and telling me they felt overwhelmed.

As Eric Garton and his colleagues found in their research, outlined in a 2017 *Harvard Business Review* article entitled 'Employee Burnout Is a Problem with the Company, Not the Person',

'In one company we studied, the average manager was losing one

day a week to email and other electronic communications and two days a week to meetings. The highly talented managers will lose even more time to collaboration as their overwork earns them more responsibility and an even larger workload.'

A LITTLE SUB-MYTH ABOUT BURNOUT AND ENGAGEMENT...

A common myth is that engagement with and passion towards your profession and burnout are at opposite ends of the spectrum. But you can be highly engaged with your work *and* be burned out. Data from a Yale research study in 2018 showed that one in five employees reported both high engagement *and* high burnout. They felt passionate about their work, but they also felt high levels of frustration and stress. Incidentally, this group also had the highest intentions of leaving their profession or organisation—even higher than the unengaged group that was studied. The former were highly dedicated, but they were *also* highly burned out.

Take Jenny, for instance—a high-performing surgeon who we interviewed for this book. She had a stellar track-record of success but, over the course of several years, had sunk into burnout. Even when she was suffering an extreme level of burnout, which was taking an enormous toll on her physical and emotional wellbeing, she *still* loved her job and did not want to leave her profession. As she pointed out, 'I wanted to keep doing my job, which I really love. If I had been worried at any point about patient safety, I would've stopped. But I wasn't getting the same sense of satisfaction about what I was doing. I never felt like I was good enough, but I didn't feel bad enough to not be doing it.'

When you look at the Yale study, and Jenny's experience, it goes some way to debunk the myth that low performers and those who are disengaged with their profession make up the bulk of the burned-out. This reality has interesting implications for professions where there are strong altruistic motivations, such as medicine or social work.

The 2020 Cogo Workplace Wellbeing Survey found some interesting insights into the relationship between engagement, professional efficacy and exhaustion among Kiwis and Aussies, too. It seems you can still believe you're delivering good work while feeling exhausted—58 per cent of those showing no signs of reduced professional efficacy (one of the main symptoms of burnout) did, however, show signs of exhaustion. Additionally, you can still be engaged in your work despite feeling exhausted—34 per cent of those showing no signs of a lack of engagement did, however, show signs of exhaustion.

MYTH THREE: JUST TAKE A FEW DAYS OFF AND YOU'LL BE RIGHT

A third common myth that circles the halls of many organisations, and the minds of many people, is that all you need to do to get over burnout is to take a holiday or a couple of days off and it'll all be tickety-boo.

Yes—and no.

Rest and a complete break *can* help people start the process of recovering from burnout. But it's not enough on its own. Sometimes it's not enough, period.

One of the common markers that someone is suffering from burnout is that they'll take a break or go on holiday but return to work just as exhausted. Their tank can't fill up. Their batteries can't recharge. They're still exhausted, despite the break. Burnout can't be solved merely by taking a holiday.

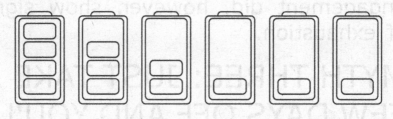

In a 2018 American Psychological Association survey of more than 1500 US workers, two-thirds of respondents said that the mental benefits of a vacation had disappeared within a few days of their return. Similarly, a 1997 study of 76 clerical employees in Israel, published in the *Journal of Applied Psychology*, found that the workers' self-reported feelings of burnout had bounced back to their pre-vacation levels within three weeks of taking a break.

Consider Amanda, a successful professional who suffered from burnout. Although she didn't recognise it at the time, she had been sliding into burnout for over a year. When she took a break for several weeks to recover from an operation, she was sure the feelings of exhaustion and cynicism she'd been experiencing at work would go away. The opposite occurred. After only a few weeks back in her role, she felt even worse.

'Well, I didn't really notice it [the burnout]. That's the thing. I took time off to have an operation, and as I got towards the last week or so of my three weeks off, well, something in the brain starts working. I realised I actually didn't want to go back to part of my

work. And I said to myself, "What in the hell is going on?"

'*And then, I started thinking about my life. I went back to work, and I realised the same patterns were happening. I went back to work to see whether it was just about changing my lifestyle—like doing a little bit of meditation, doing yoga, doing some other stuff like that. But then, everything just kind of went back to the same.*'

Remember the fish in the contaminated water? The myth that a holiday will fix the problem is just like expecting the fish to get better, despite it being plopped back into that same water after a break. If we continue to put burned-out people back into an organisation with exactly the same conditions, it's unlikely you'll see them rebounding any time soon. It sounds simplistic, and it is—if nothing has changed, then nothing will change.

The last common myth I'll cover has a grain of truth in it, but it's not the whole picture...

MYTH FOUR: BURNOUT IS CAUSED PURELY BY STRESS OR BY WORKING LONG HOURS

Let's break these two myths down separately, starting with stress.

Stress in and of itself doesn't cause burnout.

Eustress, the term for *positive* stress, coined by endocrinologist Hans Selye, is actually beneficial to us. Eustress is when we're pushed slightly outside of our comfort zone but we're not overwhelmed. This 'positive stress' fosters higher performance and increases our motivation—it's the good stuff. The right amount of stress is a good thing for our performance. Too much (or too little) stress is when performance (and usually the human who's performing the work) suffers.

However, it's not just the *amount* of stress we experience that can lead to burnout. It's also *how long we experience that stress for.* Long-term exposure to high amounts of stress is more likely to lead to burnout, especially when it's combined with other factors. You don't get burned out by one short—even highly intense—period of high stress.

For example, you might be working on a project with an intense workload for a finite time, yet there's still an end in sight. Or you might be a healthcare professional, police officer, firefighter or someone in human services who deals regularly with trauma and high-stress situations. These short, intense bursts of stress aren't going to result in burnout.

But let's take that same professional in human services. Constantly encountering high-stress situations, without the resources to manage them sufficiently, where you're also experiencing unfair treatment at work or an unmanageable workload (all causes of burnout), means the chances of experiencing burnout suddenly rise steeply.

Take Lucy, for instance. In her case, experiencing high stress over a period of time contributed significantly to her burnout.

'When I woke up every morning hating to go to a job that I previously had happily gone to at 7am and stayed there till 8pm, you know, dreading waking up in the morning, that's when I knew something was wrong ... To give an indication of the stress—I used to use two or three computers at once. I dealt with all the customers, I would tell the accountant stuff—I did everything, I ran the place! Then when I left, it took two and a half staff members to replace me, and they still couldn't do what I did.'

It's when we experience *chronic, long-term, high levels of stress* that it's likely that burnout will take hold.

The Cogo survey saw a big jump in the rates of exhaustion, isolation, depersonalisation and reduced engagement (major indicators of burnout) in those experiencing stress at work more than once a week, compared with those experiencing stress at work between once a week and once a month. Their findings therefore suggest that persistent, high-frequency stress is the issue here. The study showed:

- only 35 per cent of those experiencing stress at work between once a week and a few times a month showed signs of exhaustion, but 85 per cent of those experiencing stress at work more than once a week showed signs (making those experiencing stress at work more than once a week 2.4 times more likely to show signs of exhaustion)
- only 13 per cent of those experiencing stress at work between once a week and a few times a month showed signs of isolation, but 44 per cent of those experiencing stress at work more than once a week showed signs (so those experiencing stress at work more than once a week were 3.4 times more likely to show signs of isolation)
- only 16 per cent of those experiencing stress at work between once a week and a few times a month showed signs of depersonalisation, but 45 per cent

of those experiencing stress at work more than once a week showed signs (meaning those experiencing stress at work more than once a week were three times as likely to show signs of depersonalisation)

- 40 per cent of those experiencing stress at work between once a week and a few times a month showed signs of a lack of engagement, but 77 per cent of those experiencing stress at work more than once a week showed signs (so those experiencing stress at work more than once a week were twice as likely to show signs of a lack of engagement).

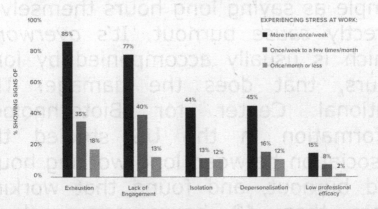

Figure 1: Share of survey respondents showing signs of exhaustion, lack of engagement, isolation, depersonalisation and low professional efficacy split by the frequency with which they

experience stress at work (Cogo Workplace Wellbeing Survey 2020)

Now let's look at the 'burnout is caused by long hours' argument.

Once again, long hours in and of themselves *do not necessarily cause burnout.* But there's a link. When we work long hours over a long time, and those long hours are combined with other burnout-causing factors (such as a lack of resources or little control over the job you're charged with), then the chance of burnout increases.

Studies have shown that while working long hours is significantly correlated with burnout, it's not as simple as saying long hours themselves directly *cause* burnout. It's *overwork,* which is usually accompanied by long hours, that does the damage. The National Center for Biotechnology Information in the US studied the association between long working hours and burnout, and found that working more than 40 hours per week is correlated with burnout. The association is even stronger when people work more than 60 hours per week.

Shift work has also been shown to increase burnout. In one study of 2772 healthcare workers in Thailand, burnout was found more frequently among shift workers than those who did not work shifts. If you're a leader of shift workers, then you obviously need to be cognisant of burnout.

*

In summary, it's important that we work to separate fact from fiction when it comes to burnout and dispel damaging myths in our organisations. If we don't do this, then we'll continue to make poor decisions that lead to costly outcomes. Decision-making that is based on these myths can needlessly damage people's careers and continue to create the 'contaminated water' that causes burnout in the first place.

KEY TAKEOUTS

Burnout is predominantly an organisational problem, not an individual one. Recognising this is key to how we tackle it.

- Anyone can experience burnout. It doesn't only happen to non-performers—and if you suffer from burnout, it doesn't mean you're weak. In fact, high performers can be more at risk of burnout, partly because of their organisation's response to their performance. You can even have feelings of high engagement towards your work and your profession and be burned out at the same time.
- Burnout can't be solved by taking a holiday or a short break from work. In fact, if your batteries don't recharge after taking a break, that is a warning sign that you might have burnout.
- Stress in and of itself is not bad. In fact, the right amount of stress is good for performance and engagement. It's when that stress is chronic and extreme that burnout is more likely to occur.
- Working long hours does not necessarily cause burnout in itself (although there is a correlation). What does cause burnout is chronic, long-term, excessive workplace stress.

Overwork causes stress, and working long hours is usually associated with overwork.

A proper understanding of the phenomenon of burnout is another good starting point for tackling these myths. In the next chapter, we take a look at what burnout is—and, perhaps, more importantly, what it *isn't*.

CHAPTER 3
WHAT IS BURNOUT?

'Pressure is a positive in a business environment, but prolonged exposure to pressure is when you get problems.'
Ben Willmot, head of public policy, CIPD (Chartered Institute of Personnel and Development, UK)

When I was 28, I became part-owner of a recruitment firm in a management buyout, and was promoted to the leadership team, of which I was the youngest person. It heralded a period when I experienced higher levels of stress than I'd ever experienced before. I was leading a larger team than I had previously, getting my head around being a member of a senior leadership team for the first time, and heading up some big projects as the economy and our business grew quickly. There were moments when I felt overwhelmed, stressed and well outside my comfort zone.

However, the main emotions I felt at the time were those of excitement and positivity. It might have felt like I was whitewater rafting out of control most of the time, but it was also a lot of fun!

Fast forward to when I was experiencing burnout and had my 'Nicholas no-hug' moment. This was a completely different experience and set of circumstances, with different feelings. This time, I had less control over the work, partly due to nonnegotiable directives coming from a far-off US head office. The stress was exacerbated by having to lead my team through the global financial crisis (GFC). I was juggling motherhood and a full-time role on a part-time basis, while still delivering on client projects—all the while leading a restructure and dealing with the associated redundancies. I felt exhausted beyond belief, cynical (which until then had been a completely foreign emotion to me at work), disillusioned and drained of any positive emotion. Rather than white-water rafting, it felt like my boat had too many holes in it for me to plug, and that I was sinking.

In both instances there was workplace stress—but the type, level and duration of that stress was very different. In the earlier scenario, I wasn't sure I could succeed, but felt optimistic, and had the resources and level of control to meet the challenge. In the latter, I felt almost sure I *couldn't* succeed, and that made me feel hopeless and exhausted. In short, one of these experiences led to the experience of burnout, while the other one didn't.

As we've seen in the previous chapter, and through my story here, stress in and of itself doesn't cause burnout. There were differences in each of my scenarios that reflect the research on burnout. In the first situation, I had distinct clarity on what my role was, and I had the resources to do it. I was also surrounded by supportive peers in the same office.

In the second situation there was less clarity, too many priorities and not enough resources. I had an amazing boss, but he was based in a different location and was often travelling. Remote leadership was the name of the game. Although I had wonderful peers, they too were in different offices, leading different business units with their own challenges. So I felt a lot more isolated.

High stress was present in both situations—but again, there were clear differences. No doubt there were other factors which led the second scenario to end in burnout and not the first, but the factors I have listed here played a significant part.

It's important that we understand what exactly burnout is (and perhaps more importantly, what it is *not*) if we want to reduce it in our workplaces. So in this chapter, we look at the key differences (and the similarities) between burnout, stress and depression—and we explore why stress in and of itself is not the problem. In fact, I'll show you how a certain amount of stress is actually *better,* not worse, for performance and wellbeing.

WHAT EXACTLY IS BURNOUT? IS IT JUST

FEELING STRESSED AND TIRED?

Burnout is a state of emotional, physical and mental exhaustion caused by excessive and prolonged stress related to your professional life. The World Health Organization (WHO) has recently come out and defined burnout as an occupational phenomenon.

'What's the big deal about that?', you might be wondering. Well, it's a big deal because it's an indication that burnout is on the rise and is enough of a problem for this specialised agency of the United Nations to make a formal definition. It's also an indication that burnout is having a greater negative impact globally than ever before.

As the WHO put it, 'Once we recognize burnout for the pandemic it is, we can begin the journey towards healthier and happier lives and work.' By defining burnout as an occupational phenomenon, the WHO hopes to increase awareness, which will enable people to get help earlier. And it will change the way we view burnout in the workplace.

Here's the World Health Organization's definition of burnout:

> *'Burnout is a syndrome conceptualized as resulting from chronic workplace stress that has not been successfully managed. It is characterized by three dimensions:*
>
> *—feelings of energy depletion or exhaustion;*
>
> *—increased mental distance from one's job, or feelings of negativism or cynicism related to one's job; and*
>
> *—reduced professional efficacy.*
>
> *Burnout refers specifically to phenomena in the occupational context and should not be applied to describe experiences in other areas of life.'*

WHAT BURNOUT IS NOT

It's worth starting with what burnout is *not*. This chart gives you a useful and quick comparison:

Burnout is not this...	Burnout is more like this...
- Everyday stress - Feeling tired after a period of intense activity or a stressful situation - Something from which you rebound after a weekend off or a holiday - Caused by factors outside the workplace - Depression (but there's a correlation — see the sections that follow) - Something that happens overnight - Days when you feel exhausted, depleted or unmotivated	- Prolonged, high-level workplace stress - Chronic exhaustion - Still feeling exhausted after taking a break - Specifically related to and caused by work/occupational factors - Has some similar symptoms to depression, but is work-specific - A gradual process - You feel exhausted, depleted and unmotivated all or most of the time

So, you might be thinking, I feel stressed out. Am I suffering from burnout?

Not necessarily. It's unlikely you're suffering from burnout if you've experienced a stressful day, or even a stressful week. You are unlikely to be suffering from burnout if you have a month-long project that has high stress-related activity, requiring you to work long hours (although it is possible to have burnout in this circumstance, depending on the severity of the stress, combined with other burnout-causing factors). Experiencing challenging periods of high stress at work do not mean you are suffering from burnout.

Burnout is not just feeling stressed out. It's not even experiencing bouts of feeling completely swamped. At times you might feel unable to cope with work-related stress—but then it subsides. Burnout is likely to happen when you experience chronic, sustained and long-term stress at work. It's when that feeling of drowning under work-related stress doesn't subside. It stays constant and unrelenting—and, in some cases, it gets worse. It's at the extreme end of the stress scale. It's chronic and it feels unremitting.

Although stress can be experienced in all areas of our lives—we can feel stressed out about our finances or our personal relationships, for example—burnout is exclusively the domain of the workplace. *It's work-related stress only*. So if you are experiencing high stress in your personal life, that's tough-going, but it's not burnout.

STRESS, EUSTRESS AND THE 'INVERTED U' MODEL

The word 'stress' comes from the Latin word 'strictus' and means 'drawn tight'. 'Drawn tight' can be a positive state—like when we draw the bow in an arrow, or when an athlete's muscles contract before they start a race. In fact, as we saw earlier, 'eustress' is a term which refers to a positive response you have to a particular stressor. Eustress is both useful and desirable in the workplace.

Eustress, or positive stress, has the following characteristics:
- It motivates us and focuses our energy.
- It's short term.
- It is perceived as being within our coping abilities.
- It feels exciting.
- It improves performance.

Distress, on the other hand, as the name implies, is stress that we deem to be negative. This is the bad stress that can be harmful to not only our minds but also our bodies. If it's left unchecked, and if it's present over a long period of time, it can cause burnout.

Distress, or negative stress, has the following characteristics:
- It causes us anxiety or concern.
- It can be either short or long term.
- It's perceived as outside of our coping abilities.
- It feels unpleasant.
- It decreases our performance.
- It can lead to mental and physical issues.

Think of a time when a task you performed at work required a good deal of exertion, concentration and output—maybe it was a major presentation or a time when you had just been promoted into a new role. It's likely you were sufficiently outside your comfort zone to have to make an extra effort to perform well. You probably felt some butterflies and weren't entirely sure of your ability. You might even have had a touch of imposter syndrome, when you doubt your accomplishments or talents and have a persistent internalised fear of being exposed as a 'fraud'. But all this made you try harder and focus even more.

Now, think of a task at work that you can do in your sleep and that requires very little exertion or concentration. There's no stress at all when it comes to performing this particular task. Now think about what it would be like if your whole job was made up of tasks like this. What might that lead to? What feelings or responses might you experience? Yep, you guessed it—boredom, frustration, inattention. It's certainly unlikely to lead to your best performance. In fact, our mistakes and accidents tend to *increase* when we encounter these situations. This isn't ideal when we look at this through a health and safety lens.

Boredom has been associated with a range of negative outcomes, including poor performance at work, accidents, absenteeism, errors, increased risk-taking/thrill-seeking, sleepiness, stress-related health problems such as heart attacks, job dissatisfaction and even property damage.

But too much stress is not good for us or our performance, either. This 'too much stress' might come in the form of experiencing stress for long periods of time or it might be pervasive—overwork might be the cultural norm in your organisation or profession. The excessive stress may come from not having the resources required to perform your job well. These are all things that push people to the wrong end of the stress continuum.

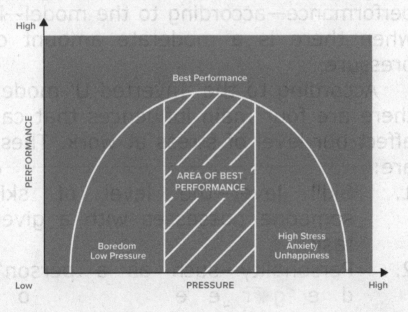

The 'Inverted U' model (also known as Yerkes-Dodson Law) was created by psychologists Robert Yerkes and John Dodson way back in 1908, so it's been around for a while. It illustrates the relationship between pressure (or arousal) and performance caused by stress.

If we don't experience enough pressure, it's likely to result in boredom, low performance and a lack of engagement. If there's too much pressure, you start to see negative consequences like high levels of anxiety, stress and burnout. The ideal amount of pressure for best performance—according to the model—is when there is a moderate amount of pressure.

According to the 'Inverted U' model, there are four main influences that can affect our level of stress at work. These are:
1. Skill level—the level of skill someone possesses with a given task
2. Personality—such as a person's degree of extroversion/introversion, and how well that aligns to the job they are required to do
3. Trait anxiety—a person's 'self-talk', such as that associated with self-confidence and self-efficacy

4. Task complexity—the level of attention and effort that a person has to put into a task in order to complete it successfully.

The key takeout (especially for leaders) when it comes to this model is to consider these aspects when delegating work or assigning tasks to individual team members. It's also important to be aware of where the organisation or team tends to operate overall when it comes to pressure on this curve.

OUR RESPONSE TO STRESS MATTERS

Another factor to take into account when looking at stress and burnout is our *response* to stress. Whether we subjectively view a particular stressor as good or bad makes a difference. Viewing something as a challenge or a threat can change the way we respond to it.

According to a massive research study at the University of Wisconsin, published in 2011, our attitudes about stress have a significant impact on its effects. It turns out that *stressing about stress* increases its serious implications for our health and wellbeing.

However, although this is an important point to make when we're discussing whether stress is a good or a bad thing, it in no way suggests that if you just buck up and be positive, or try to 'work through' chronic, pervasive stress at work, you won't suffer from burnout. That is definitely not the case. But it does have implications for how we frame up stress for ourselves and our teams.

In summary, stress in and of itself is not bad. In fact, in the right doses and frequency, stress is good for us at work. It's when the stress becomes chronic, extreme, is part of the fabric of doing our job or when it comes in high doses over a long period of time that it causes issues and can lead to burnout.

WHAT IS THE DIFFERENCE BETWEEN DEPRESSION AND BURNOUT?

The first researcher to coin the phrase 'burnout', psychologist Herbert Freudenberger, said that burnout 'looks like depression.'

When people talk about depression and burnout, they often couple the two together. The two are sometimes even used interchangeably. The symptoms of depression and burnout can *look* similar—for example, impaired concentration and loss of interest—but they're not the same thing.

Although there continues to be debate amongst researchers as to *how* they're different, the current consensus is that they are distinct but related. For example, a 2019 meta-analysis study by Panagiota Koutsimani, Anthony Montgomery and Katerina Georganta, examining the relationship between burnout and depression, revealed no conclusive overlap between burnout and depression—indicating that they are indeed different and robust constructs.

But at the same time, there *is* a relationship between the two—experiencing depression can make you more susceptible to burnout, and burnout at the extreme end of the scale *can* and *does* often lead to depression and other mental illnesses.

So, let's delve into the similarities and differences between depression and burnout.

HOW ARE BURNOUT AND DEPRESSION SIMILAR?

The symptoms of burnout and depression can *present* similarly. For example, a person experiencing depression and a person experiencing burnout will often both demonstrate a loss of interest and a lack of concentration, as well as physical symptoms such as insomnia, headaches and gastrointestinal issues. Both burnout and depression have been associated with impaired work performance, absenteeism and job turnover.

Although its *cause* is specifically work related, the *symptoms and the effects of burnout* usually spill over into a person's personal life. For example, the feelings of cynicism and detachment people have about their work when they're suffering from burnout can extend to family and friends, not just towards co-workers or customers. We don't operate in isolation—what we are experiencing has a knock-on effect on those around us. Feelings of extreme exhaustion and a lack of self-efficacy at work will almost certainly affect other parts of the sufferer's life.

HOW ARE BURNOUT AND DEPRESSION DIFFERENT?

Burnout has three specific symptoms—exhaustion, cynicism (or depersonalisation) and loss of efficacy related to your job. While these might also show up in someone experiencing depression, they are not the *only* symptoms of depression. There are others at play.

One of the biggest differences between burnout and depression is the root cause. It's worth reiterating that burnout is *specifically related to the workplace.* Depression is not. Depression also has other contributing factors, such as environmental and genetic influences. Although the causes of depression may be varied and complex (and may or may not have linkages to work), the cause of burnout always sits squarely in the occupational realm. Its origin is work.

'In short, burnout is a crisis in employees' psychological connection with work,' according to psychologist Michael Leiter, who along with Christina Maslach, who we mentioned earlier, is considered one of the world's foremost experts on burnout.

It's the connection of that psychological crisis to our work that's the important point here—and it illustrates one of the differences between depression and burnout.

The final word should be left to Paula Davis-Laack, founder of the American Stress & Resilience Institute:

'The prevailing belief is that about 20 percent of burnout cases can be explained by depression, and vice versa. But that means that 80

percent of the time, other factors are at play.'

KEY TAKEOUTS:

• Stress is not burnout. In fact, stress is a positive thing in the right doses. Whether we view it as a positive or a negative thing can also have an impact on our experience of stress.

• Prolonged chronic stress related to work, however, can and does lead to burnout. It's the level and duration of the work stress that's important here.

• Depression is not burnout, although the two share similar symptoms and are linked. Extreme burnout has been shown to lead to depression.

In the next chapter we delve into who is most at risk of suffering from burnout. You might be surprised...

CHAPTER 4

WHO IS MOST AT RISK OF BURNOUT?

'No matter what job you do, if you are pushed beyond your ability to cope for long periods of time, you're likely to suffer burnout.'
Michael Musker, senior research fellow at the South Australian Health and Medical Research Institute

So who is most at risk of suffering from burnout? A better question to ask might be, 'Which organisational conditions are more likely to create burnout?'

Christina Maslach, a global expert on burnout, has likened the burned-out employee to the canary in a coal mine:

'The canary in the cage goes down in the coal mine, and if the canary is having trouble breathing and functioning, it's a sign to you that the workplace, the mine, is dangerous. Too many toxic fumes,

you'd better not send people down there. It's a warning sign, and this is really what burnout is in a sense. It's a warning-sign of a toxic work environment'

However, at the same time it is useful to explore who may be most at risk of burnout. This not only goes some way to debunk unhelpful myths or assumptions and increase our general awareness of this important topic, but it also enables us to better support those who might be most at risk within our organisations and professions.

In this chapter, we take a closer look at the question 'Who is *most* at risk of burnout?' We do this from a number of different angles: gender, age, personality, occupation and hierarchical level within an organisation.

ANYONE CAN SUFFER FROM BURNOUT

When I began to delve into this question of who is most at risk of burnout, I found the answer wasn't cut and dried. In fact, I was left thinking there was definitely an opportunity for more research in this space. For many areas, such as gender, the research is mixed. For other areas, there appears to be virtually no research at all! In some cases, the jury seemed to be out as to any definitive conclusions, with some research contradicting other studies.

This is why the Cogo Workplace Wellbeing Survey is so important, because it's New Zealand-and Australia-specific, so offers valuable and relevant insights into this important field. This 2020 survey reported differences in the various signs of burnout between male and female respondents, and between occupations and positions within organisations. But burnout was by no means constrained to one occupation type or position within New Zealand and Australian organisations, according to the study.

Studies show that organisational and environmental factors have by far the biggest impact on—and are the biggest predictor of—whether or not someone experiences burnout. That's one thing researchers and experts in this field agree on.

But individual factors such as demographic, personality characteristics and attitudes also play a part when it comes to who is most likely to suffer from burnout.

There are some surprises, as well as some confirmed assumptions amid the research. But before we dive in, it's worth repeating: anyone can experience burnout when they have elevated stress levels, experience overwork, become exhausted or feel unappreciated or devalued in the workplace.

Let's first take a look at a question I get asked a lot: does gender play a role in burnout?

GENDER AND BURNOUT—WHO SUFFERS THE MOST?

When it comes to gender and burnout, the jury's still out. A 2010 meta study of over 400 studies revealed very little difference between genders when it comes to burnout. However, some more recent studies indicate that women may be more likely to suffer from burnout than men.

For instance, one study from Montreal University of more than 2000 workers from over 60 workplaces, which looked at the three key measures of burnout—exhaustion, cynicism and professional effectiveness—found that overall, women reported significantly higher levels of emotional exhaustion, low professional efficacy and total burnout. In this same study, however, there were two areas that were gender-neutral when it came to contributing to burnout—job insecurity and a feeling of a lack of fairness at work. Things like job insecurity and feeling a lack of fairness suck, regardless of your gender, it would seem. The 2020 Cogo research also found that, across all the signs of burnout, New Zealand and Australian women scored highest. But Cogo flagged that this may be related to the professions and positions the women in their samples were holding, and say that if a survey were to collect data about one particular profession or position, we might see something else.

So why is it that women may be more susceptible to burnout, according to more recent studies? It likely has to do with women tending to have less control over their work. And why is *that?* They are less likely to be in positions of power. Therefore, they're at risk of possessing less authority and decision-making power in the workplace.

The grim statistics on the lack of women at the top table and in leadership positions in New Zealand are well documented and make for concerning reading. According to the 2018 Grant Thornton International Women in Business Annual Report, 56 per cent of businesses had no women in senior management roles, compared with 37 per cent the year prior. Given that one of the causes of burnout is a lack of control over how we perform our jobs, you can start to see the correlation in these statistics.

So given there's a lot of contention about men and women and who is more prone to burnout, it might be more useful to take a look at the differences in what contributes to stress in the Australasian workplace for men and women. Here's what the Cogo study showed us...

The top five factors contributing to a feeling of stress at work for male respondents were:
- 54 per cent 'the nature of my work'
- 40 per cent 'work politics or bureaucracy'
- 35 per cent 'an unrealistically high workload'
- 27 per cent 'the possibility of losing my job or business'
- 27 per cent 'challenges due to the Covid-19 pandemic'.

The top five factors contributing to a feeling of stress at work for female respondents were:
- 50 per cent 'work politics or bureaucracy'
- 45 per cent 'the nature of my work'
- 44 per cent 'an unrealistically high workload'
- 37 per cent 'the behaviour of my manager/management'
- 35 per cent 'the behaviour of my co-workers'.

When we look at these results, the top three factors are the same. But it appears that women are more likely to be stressed by the behaviour of others than men are.

Although men and women report similar average stress levels across different studies, women are more likely than men to report that their stress levels are on the rise.

One interesting outcome of studies on burnout is the finding that men and women tend to *experience* burnout in different ways. For instance, women are more likely to suffer from emotional exhaustion, while men are more likely to experience cynicism or depersonalisation. Other studies indicate that women might be more likely to *express* feelings of emotional and physical fatigue (such as emotional exhaustion), because they have learned to display their emotions, whereas men are more likely to shut off and withdraw under stress (i.e. depersonalisation), because they have learned to conceal theirs. This is in line with other research on stress and gender, which shows that men and women report different reactions to stress, both physically and mentally.

However, both the general public and trained professionals alike tend to associate emotion-expressive behaviours with psychological distress, whereas emotion-suppressive behaviours tend to be associated with strength, masculinity and psychological adjustment. This suggests that men's burnout may be more likely to go unrecognised.

The danger associated with this trend is that it helps perpetuate the myths that women are more 'burned-out' than men and that men are more resilient to stress than women, which isn't actually the case. This is important, because a commonly held view that women experience burnout more than men may work to enforce stereotypes and encourage implicit and explicit gender discrimination against women. It could also be damaging to men, as their burnout experiences may go unacknowledged, meaning they remain unsupported and untreated.

Those from the LGBTQ community may be even more at risk. Employees who are more likely to experience discrimination and harassment in the workplace are also more likely to experience feelings of isolation—a major cause of burnout.

Finally, 'age and stage' of life cycle may also contribute to a person being prone to burnout, it would appear. The Montreal University study I mentioned at the beginning of this section suggests that burnout symptoms vary greatly according to the different life stages of working men and women. Younger men, and women aged 20–35 and 55 years and over, are particularly susceptible, making these age groups a good place to start with targeted programmes to reduce the risk of burnout.

DOES PERSONALITY PLAY A PART?

You might be wondering if personality plays a part in burnout. Before I answer this question, I want to reiterate—along with most authors on this topic—that burnout is far more of a social phenomenon than an individual one. I'll say it again: anyone can (and does) suffer from burnout. Environmental and external factors play a far bigger role in burnout prevalence than internal factors such as personality.

That said, the research (unsurprisingly) shows some links between certain personality traits and burnout. For instance, if you have perfectionistic tendencies, you're more at risk, according to the research. Ditto with being a Type A personality, rather than a Type B personality. (Although these terms imply a personality typology, it's more like a trait continuum, with extremes of Type-A and Type-B individuals on each end.)

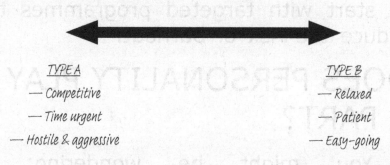

TYPE A
— Competitive
— Time urgent
— Hostile & aggressive

TYPE B
— Relaxed
— Patient
— Easy-going

Traits such as levels of extroversion, self-efficacy and self-esteem have an impact on burnout rates too. Research by Gabriella Gustafsson at Umea University in Sweden, for example, found that emotional stability, mental alertness, confidence and power are predictors or precursors of burnout. How people respond to stressors and work settings is different according to their personality characteristics, so it makes sense that burnout rates are also affected by this.

Those people who have higher job expectations overall—including wanting to achieve success at work—are more prone to burnout. Low self-esteem and lower emotional stability, greater competitiveness, an excessive need for control and high levels of conscientiousness have all been found to statistically increase the chances of a person experiencing burnout.

In short, individual differences play a small but measurable role in whether someone is likely to experience burnout. That said, rather than getting too caught up in this question, it's better to focus our attention on the big levers that make a difference to whether people suffer from burnout in our workplaces. And that's the external environment; leadership, work culture and organisational processes are much more significant than a person's individual personality or gender.

Before we move on to consider the causes of burnout, and the role those external environmental factors play, let's examine one more question for insights about the prevalence of burnout...

WHAT ABOUT DIFFERENT PROFESSIONS?

Are some professions more susceptible to burnout than others? This is where things get interesting.

While personality might be a more minor factor in accounting for differences in burnout rates, and there are mixed results when it comes to gender in the current research, studies have shown overwhelmingly that certain professions are more prone to burnout than others. And, when we dig into the causes of burnout, the reasons behind this make sense.

Here are the professions most at risk of burnout, according to research.

HUMAN SERVICES PROFESSIONALS, 'HELPING' PROFESSIONALS AND

EMERGENCY SERVICE WORKERS

Human services professionals and 'helping' professionals are more at risk of burnout than the general public. This includes social workers, caregivers and mental health practitioners.

People working in this field often have to cope with emotionally demanding relationships with those in their care—and there's a definite link between emotional labour and burnout. These professions feature more highly in the burnout statistics than others, such as manufacturing, for instance. It's little wonder that the challenging realities and personal distress that those in some of these professions face on a daily basis leave them more prone to burnout.

Emergency service workers such as police, medics, firefighters and emergency medical practitioners all fall into this camp, too. Emergency service workers are subject to acute, emotionally demanding situations as a key part of their job. In other words, before you add in any of the systemic or cultural factors that cause burnout, they're already disadvantaged by the nature of the work that they do.

THE MEDICAL PROFESSION

A recent US study of over 15,000 US doctors found that 44 per cent were experiencing symptoms of burnout. Closer to home, in New Zealand, nearly half of our doctors have considered leaving medicine because of burnout, a survey has found.

A survey of 300 Kiwi doctors by the Medical Protection Society found half felt unable to take a break between procedures, and almost as many did not feel their wellbeing was a priority at work.

Specialty emergency medicine doctors, surgeons, general practitioners (GPs) and interns feature particularly highly in burnout figures. For example, recent research looking at burnout in surgeons showed that 56 per cent of surgeons were experiencing burnout—that's *over half!*

This propensity for medical professionals to experience burnout at a higher rate than the general population can be attributed, in part, to the demands and stress of patient care, long hours and the increasing administrative burdens associated with practising medicine. A lack of resources may also contribute to these high figures, along with an expectation that 'long hours are just part of the job'. Many of the medical professionals I interviewed for this book worked over 60 hours a week; this was the norm.

> *'I work 60 hours a week. I do two full weeks with a weekend in the middle of those two weeks where I am available for any emergencies for 96 hours. I am also responsible over those 96 hours for all surgical inpatients for the hospital. I do admin work mostly at night, I sit there typing and working and carrying on. And so I think it prevents me from paying full attention to my children when I get home as much as I want to.'*
> Jenny, surgeon

THE LEGAL PROFESSION

The legal profession is synonymous with high workloads, high-pressure deadlines and long hours. And it also features in the burnout statistics—but not in a good way!

The New Zealand College of Law Performance and Well-Being Study 2019 revealed some pretty scary statistics—91 per cent of lawyers have experienced burnout. Over half of New Zealand lawyers have experienced burnout within the past month. And two in five lawyers believe doing more meaningful work would reduce levels of stress and burnout.

There was some good news in this survey, however. The number of those reporting burnout is trending downwards, with a significantly lower number saying they have experienced burnout in the past month compared with levels seen in 2018.

Worryingly, though, over three in five lawyers (62 per cent) think that their workplace could do more to reduce employee stress. In particular, younger lawyers (80 per cent), those in large law firms (82 per cent) and those in more junior roles think that their workplace could be doing more.

THE TEACHING PROFESSION

'I am an ECE teacher. In this profession it is the expectation to plan, reflect, buy resources, keep up with continual professional development, goal setting and paperwork—all outside your scheduled eight hours a day—that causes constant stress. Work NEVER ends.'
Anonymous respondent, Cogo Workplace Wellbeing Survey 2020

The teaching profession also figures prominently in burnout figures, and it gets worse for those teachers in leadership roles. For example, in one study conducted by the National Association of Elementary School Principals in the US, as many as 75 per cent of elementary school principals demonstrated burnout symptoms.

The sobering results of the 2020 Cogo Workplace Wellbeing Survey painted just as concerning a trend around burnout and the New Zealand teaching profession. As we can see in the graph on the next page, education professionals were most likely to show signs of exhaustion (86 per cent) and depersonalisation (71 per cent)—much higher than those others surveyed in the study. Both exhaustion and depersonalisation are key symptoms of burnout, so we need to do more to support our teachers in the critical role they do in educating our children.

> *'I have decided to quit my teaching job. Ever since I made this decision I have felt as though a huge weight has been lifted off me. I will have to re-train, and the job market is awful, but I cannot go on like this. I love teaching, but I hate being a teacher in NZ secondary schools. I am physically and psychologically unwell because of this job.'*

Anonymous respondent, Cogo Workplace Wellbeing Survey, 2020

Finally, here's what the Cogo research showed when it came to burnout and various professions:

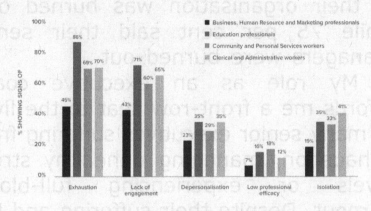

Figure 2: Share of survey respondents showing signs of exhaustion, lack of engagement, isolation, depersonalisation, and low professional efficacy split by profession (Cogo Workplace Wellbeing Survey 2020)

SENIOR EXECUTIVES

Although few C-suite executives would admit it, burnout at senior executive levels is more common than you might think. And the trend is growing.

A Harvard Medical School study found that some 96 per cent of senior leaders felt 'somewhat burned out' and a third described that burnout as 'extreme'. According to another 2013 study of senior managers and C-suite executives, about half thought the CEO of their organisation was burned out, while 75 per cent said their senior managers were burned out.

My role as an executive coach affords me a front-row seat to the lives of many senior executives suffering from exhaustion, managing unhealthy stress levels or experiencing full-blown burnout. Despite their suffering and the negative consequences on their health, professional and personal lives, most are (quite rightly) reticent to admit their feelings of being overwhelmed or exhausted for fear of negative repercussions on their career.

We're seeing an increase in cases of high-profile CEOs taking time off due to 'extreme fatigue', such as Lloyds Banking Group chief executive António Horta-Osório in 2011. Another high-profile executive, Jeffrey Kindler, a former CEO of Pfizer, cited burnout as the key reason for suddenly stepping down from his role in 2010. It was a risky move, but one which we need to be more transparent about if we are to address burnout at this level—and the mental health of those in charge in general.

Although there's not much research into CEO burnout (which surprises me, to be honest) I believe CEOs are prone to falling prey to one of the biggest causes of burnout: loneliness. From what I've witnessed in coaching CEOs, it's certainly lonely at the top. There's only one of you, and although you may have a board and an executive team, there are limitations to these social connections—there are things you can't and wouldn't share with either of these two stakeholder groups.

It's not just my observations as an executive coach which show this 'lonely at the top' factor playing out. A survey by RHR International, published in 2012, found that over half of CEOs report experiencing feelings of loneliness in their roles. Of this group, 61 per cent believe isolation hinders their performance. (We'll look at the role of isolation in burnout further in the next chapter, when we dive deeper into the causes.)

While big salaries are seen to compensate CEOs for the substantial stressors that go along with being the head of an organisation, the emotional exhaustion and persistent demands of diverse stakeholders in an increasingly volatile environment can potentially increase CEOs' risk of burnout—and mean that there's more stigma, if they do suffer from burnout. When a CEO takes extended time off or resigns due to stress-related causes, both markets and employees get spooked.

And the effects of burned-out people leading an organisation are significant. Although stress is seen as part and parcel of the CEO position, if the CEO is burned out, the impact on the organisation is far more profound than it would be from someone further down the hierarchy, whose impact is not as wide-ranging.

According to the Cogo research, those further down in an organisation's hierarchy experience stress differently from those at the top. This could be due to many C-level employees being somewhat buffered from the organisational politics that are felt further down in the hierarchy. An organisation's culture is predominantly set at the top table—and its effects are felt more keenly by those in the lower levels of management.

Here's what the Cogo survey found:
- Despite similar stress levels, senior staff (owners/operators/C-level executives and senior managers) are less likely to take stress leave (24 per cent, versus 32 per cent of middle managers and 41 per cent of general staff).
- Senior staff are more likely to be open about the stress they experience at work compared with general staff (60 per cent of senior staff versus just 36 per cent of general staff).
- Only 12 per cent of owner/operator/C-level respondents say that the behaviour of their co-workers contributes to their feelings of stress at work, compared with 32 per cent of general staff.
- 29 per cent of owner/C-level respondents say that work politics or bureaucracy contributes to their

feelings of stress at work, compared with 50 per cent of general staff.

'It's all very well to have some services to look after wellbeing, but no good to be so exhausted to not be bothered with them. The main issue is a lack of staff and high performance expectations. And if you look like you may get close to what is expected, the goal post moves, to make it unrealistic.'

Anonymous CEO or Managing Director respondent from Cogo Workplace Wellbeing Survey

It's important that we do more research to gain a greater understanding of CEO-or owner-level burnout. Why? Because people at this level within an organisation have a huge impact on the organisation when it comes to all facets—culture, performance and wellbeing, for starters. If those at the top are burned out, it will have wide-reaching consequences for the organisation they lead. Burnout is 'catchy'. The flow-on effects of a burned-out CEO will cascade down into the organisation. And their burnout packs a bigger punch when it comes to its impacts.

We also need to change the mental models we have about the pressure and mental distress that tend to accompany this level of role. There are unwritten but prevalent expectations on CEOs that they must operate at extremely high performance levels 100 per cent of the time, in a role which is by design, isolating. As I mentioned above, I have personally witnessed the repercussions of this level of pressure in my role as an executive coach.

It will be interesting to see what, if any, impact the experience of leading through a global pandemic and its subsequent economic impacts have on owner or CEO-levels of burnout. This will certainly be one to watch.

*

Regardless of which industry or profession you work in, if you're pushed beyond your ability to cope for long periods of time, you're more likely to suffer burnout. But, if you work in one of the professions I've outlined in this chapter, it's even more important to take serious note of both the causes and the solutions to burnout, especially if you're in a leadership role which can effect the most change.

KEY TAKEOUTS

• Anyone can suffer from burnout. Organisational factors play a much larger role in determining burnout rates than any individual factors to do with gender, personality or position.

• There are mixed results in the research when it comes to gender and burnout. Previous studies had shown no discernible difference in gender rates of burnout, but more recent studies identify more women than men suffer from burnout.

• Certain personality traits play a small but statistically significant role in whether you are susceptible to burnout.

• Certain professions and sectors feature more prominently in the burnout statistics. For example, those in the human services, medical, emergency services, teaching and legal professions are over-represented in burnout statistics.

• CEO-or owner-level burnout is an area worthy of further study, not least because the effects of a burned-out leader have a greater impact on an organisation than those further down in the organisational hierarchy.

CHAPTER 5

WHAT CAUSES BURNOUT?

'Burnout is the index of the dislocation between what people are and what they have to do. It represents an erosion in value, dignity, spirit, and will—an erosion of the human soul.'
Christina Maslach and Michael Leiter, global experts on burnout

You might think that burnout is caused by overwork—and you'd be right. This is one of the main reasons why people become burned out over time. But it's not the *only* reason. In fact, there are at least five more causes—and some of them may surprise you.

In this chapter, I'll introduce you to these other causes—insufficient rewards, isolation, a lack of control, an absence of fairness and a values conflict—and delve into overwork in more detail. We'll also explore the subtle interplay between these six primary causes of burnout—an interplay that often creates a 'perfect burnout storm' that increases the risk of burnout exponentially.

But first, it's worth taking a moment to understand human motivation, because it has a significant relationship to burnout. Without getting too technical or theoretical, a great way to do this is to take a look at Richard Ryan and Edward L. Deci's research into human motivation and the concept they came up with called Self Determination Theory (SDT).

In a nutshell, self-determination theory suggests that all of us are motivated to grow and change by three innate and universal psychological needs: competence, relatedness and autonomy. These three conditions, according to SDT, affect not only your motivation, but also your wellbeing and level of performance.

- **Competence** refers to our need to be effective when dealing with our environment.
- **Relatedness** is our need to have close, affectionate relationships with others.

- **Autonomy** refers to the need to control the course of our lives.

When any one or all three of these things are absent, it negatively impacts not only our motivation, but also our performance and wellbeing. And when these things are absent in significant or unrelenting doses, well ... cue burnout.

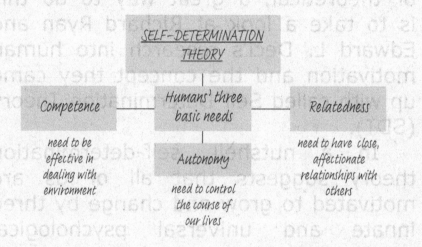

When we apply self-determination theory to our workplaces, the links between it and burnout become pretty clear, pretty quickly. You can see from the chart below which basic human psychological needs are being compromised by the causes of burnout:

Cause of burnout	Psychological need not being met
• Overwork	• Competence and autonomy
• Insufficient reward	• Competence and relatedness
• Isolation	• Relatedness
• Absence of fairness	• Autonomy and competence
• Values conflict	• Relatedness
• Lack of control	• Autonomy

THE SIX MAIN CAUSES OF BURNOUT

Through their extensive research, the world experts who I quoted earlier, Christina Maslach and Michael Leiter, have uncovered six main causes of burnout.

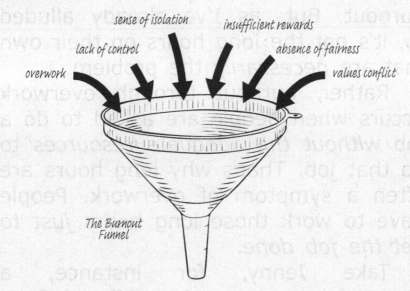

The Burnout Funnel

Now, let's delve into these causes of burnout in a little more detail. We'll start with the most obvious cause, overwork.

1. OVERWORK

> *'We would work 70 or 120 hours a week, so we would do long weekend work right through from 8 o'clock on Saturday and then not finish until 6 o'clock Monday night. And that was the norm.'*
> Simon, medical professional

Overwork is a significant cause of burnout. But, as I've already alluded to, it's not the long hours on their own that are *necessarily* the problem.

Rather, burnout through overwork occurs when people are asked to do a job *without the adequate resources* to do that job. That's why long hours are often a symptom of overwork. People have to work those long hours *just to get the job done.*

Take Jenny, for instance, a successful surgeon who suffered from burnout. She typically works 60 hours a week, then has periods where she is on call for 96 hours at a time on top of this. There are many times when she can't get done what she needs to for her role even during those hours, so she often has to work evenings and weekends on top of this to get everything completed.

What are we talking about when we refer to 'resources'? It might be unrealistic deadlines or the timeframes in which you're expected to do your job. For example, one study showed that employees who say they have enough time to do their work are 70 per cent less likely to experience burnout. It's no wonder, then, that people who are not able to gain more time, such as paramedics and firefighters, are at a higher risk of burnout. When we don't have sufficient time to get our job done, then long hours and working overtime are obvious flow-on effects.

But lack of resources is not just about time. For instance, you may not have the right equipment, people or skills required to get your job done. One client of mine was in charge of leading a team of highly specialised professionals who were in short supply; they always seemed to be working one person down. Their roles took months to fill, and he almost always had a vacancy in his team. This resulted not only in him but also his team working longer hours and with higher stress levels as they battled to meet their organisational and customer demands. There were many times when he and his team members were overworked and showing signs of burnout. It was a perfect example of overwork caused by a lack of resources (the right people, in this instance) to do the job.

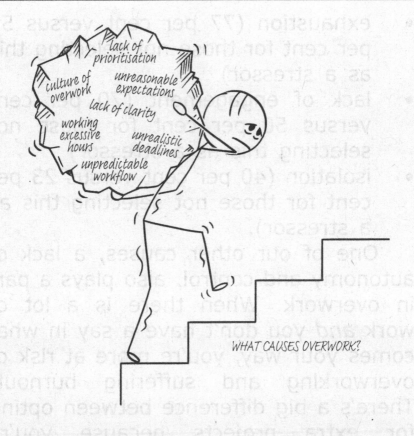

WHAT CAUSES OVERWORK?

One of the concerns when we look at overwork is that the risk of burnout jumps dramatically for those who believe they have an unrealistic workload. The Cogo Workplace Wellbeing Survey has further insights here. Of those surveyed, 39 per cent said that 'an unrealistic workload' contributed to their feelings of stress at work. Those who said this were much more likely to show signs of:

- exhaustion (77 per cent versus 51 per cent for those not selecting this as a stressor)
- lack of engagement (70 per cent versus 50 per cent for those not selecting this as a stressor)
- isolation (40 per cent versus 23 per cent for those not selecting this as a stressor).

One of our other causes, a lack of autonomy and control, also plays a part in overwork. When there is a lot of work *and* you don't have a say in what comes your way, you're more at risk of overworking and suffering burnout. There's a big difference between opting for extra projects because you're intrinsically motivated and having them thrust on you without any choice.

Other common causes of overwork include an unpredictable workflow, unrealistic deadlines or having to do fast-paced work under tight deadlines. Simon, a medical professional, spoke of these sorts of systemic demands:

> *'What you're seeing now is that in these care facilities, they're wanting their doctors to basically do a full hospital work-up. But*

urgent-care wants you to see people quickly, three to four an hour, and in general-practice you're seeing four an hour, and you don't have time to do a full work-up.'

A lack of clarity or prioritisation can also lead to overwork quicker than you can say 'burnout'. In my role as a leadership coach, a lack of prioritisation (or, rather, too many priorities) is a quick route to teams feeling not only overworked, but confused. When these overwork factors are chronic or 'baked into' the role, you're more likely to end up in a situation where burnout takes hold.

As well as causing burnout, constant overwork is also hugely demoralising! Those innate psychological needs that I referred to earlier in this chapter from the SDT model are far less likely to be met when you're struggling just to keep your head above water in order to get the job done.

Once again, without labouring the point, long hours in and of themselves may not be a problem. Someone who really enjoys working longer hours in a position that they love, where they feel like they're making progress and that they have the necessary resources to do their job, is far less at risk of burnout. However, if that same person had to work long hours *all the time* just to keep afloat of what was coming at them, and they had little control over their work or didn't have the necessary resources to do that job successfully, then the chances of overwork—and burnout—would rise. It's not the long hours *in isolation* that are necessarily the problem.

A culture of overwork

There's an underlying culture of overwork in many organisations, professions and even at a societal level in certain parts of the globe that's a growing and concerning trend. Too often, we equate 'more' with 'better'. The idea that working very long hours in order to be successful is a pervasive one, especially in certain industries and professions, like the legal and dot.com startup fields.

High-profile leaders espousing the virtues of working long hours in order to be successful also don't help. When Elon Musk says he works 80 to 90 hours a week and calls that 'pretty manageable', it fuels a cultural idea that overwork and long hours are necessary if you want to be successful. 'I'm so busy!' is worn as a badge of honour by many a stressed-out executive.

As a result, we've come to worship work and glorify working hard. Conversely, non-work is viewed as lazy. As Gary Blau, professor of human resources at Temple University's Fox School of Business, points out, 'We're headed for trouble when we assume that work is inherently virtuous and that, conversely, time off is inherently lazy.'

This culture of overwork is particularly pronounced in countries such as the United States. Recent research has revealed that the US is the most overworked developed nation in the world! But it's not just the US where overwork is a problem. In Japan, this culture of overwork has got so bad, they've invented a word for it. *Karoshi*—'death by overwork'. It is a problem so worrying that the Japanese government is working hard to address it through legislation and policy changes. This phenomenon is also widespread in South Korea, where it's referred to as *gwarosa,* and in China, overwork-induced death is called *guolaosi.*

You might be thinking that New Zealand and Australia's reputation for a more laid-back approach to work–life balance, which make us so attractive to global migrants, might mean overwork is a non-issue. But this growing culture of overwork is playing out even in the Antipodes. In one OECD Better Life Index, New Zealand had the ninth-highest percentage of employees working more than 50 hours per week, at 13.8 per cent.

As author Alex Soojung-Kim Pang so eloquently puts it in his great book *Rest—Why You Get More Done When You Work Less,* 'The challenge we face when learning to rest better is not to avoid work but to discover how to create a better fit between our work and our rest.'

Here's the absurd irony about working long hours: employee output falls sharply after a 50-hour work week. It completely tanks after 55 hours. So if you're putting in 70 hours a week, you're likely producing nothing more with those extra 15 hours. That's according to a study published in 2014 by economist John Pencavel of Stanford University. Another study showed that 'increasing a team's hours in the office by 50 per cent (from 40 to 60 hours) doesn't result in 50 per cent more output. In fact, the numbers may typically be something closer to 25–30 per cent more work in 50 percent more time.'

Sarah Green Carmichael of the *Harvard Business Review* calls it 'the story of diminishing returns ... When you overwork, you make avoidable mistakes without actually producing more.'

To add insult to irony, according to another study, managers couldn't tell the difference between employees who worked 80 hours per week and those who only pretended to. So while managers tended to punish workers who were honest about working less, there was no evidence that those employees accomplished less, nor that the overworking employees accomplished more!

Longer hours have also been connected to other troublesome organisational problems—absenteeism, employee turnover and more mistakes at work, as well as those significant declines in productivity. The costs of overwork are serious issues not just from a leadership and organisational perspective—they're pretty dire for employees themselves, too. Overwork increases the risk of heart attacks and diabetes, accelerates ageing and contributes to mental-health problems. How big of an issue is it? Stress-related health problems make up between 75 and 90 per cent of hospital visits, according to Webmed.

The role of technology and its contribution to overwork

The issue of technology and overwork is a tricky one. On one hand, technology has increased speed and efficiencies in communication. It's made us more accessible to each other. But the downside of technology is that it has also led to a greater risk of interruptions and a pressure to work outside of normal working hours.

Our 'always on' mentality, driven largely by technology, is also contributing to a culture of overwork. It's not uncommon for many executives to be expected to respond to emails at 11pm, or over the weekend. In one study, 60 per cent of workers studied used their smartphones to check in with work during the evening and on weekends. An expectation for us to be available to clients, customers or even our boss 24/7 is the norm in some professions and organisations. This can result in feeling like you're always at work—even when you're not physically there.

A study co-authored by Liuba Belkin, associate professor of management at Lehigh University in the US, found a link between an organisation's expectations around people answering emails and emotional exhaustion, a key cause of burnout. The study found that both actual time spent on emails and organisational expectations regarding employee availability to monitor work emails after-hours led to emotional exhaustion.

2. A LACK OF CONTROL

One of the worst feelings we as humans can have is a sense of having no control over what is happening to us. We despise it. And so most of our lives are spent trying to control the uncontrollable, trying to shape outcomes to what we want (which sometimes works!). But it also increases a sense of self-efficacy, and that makes us feel good about ourselves.

So strong is our need for control that feeling a lack of it can even have an impact on our physical health. In one study, researchers gave the members of one group in an aged-care facility control over which plant to grow in their room and which movies to watch. The other group was denied those options. In the eighteen-month period that followed, the death rate of the second group was *double* that of the first. (A pretty outrageous experiment!)

It's no surprise, then, that a sense of having little or no control over the work we do can be pretty stressful. And it's a big contributor to burnout. Specifically, when people feel they don't have any say in *how* they do their job, it's a powerful and nefarious combination.

For Lucy, one of the people interviewed for this book, a feeling that she had no control over her workload, driven mainly through expectations from her direct manager, contributed significantly to her burnout.

'Sometimes I would want to say, "No, I can't work late tonight, because I promised I'd be home" ... Then at 4pm my boss pops into the office with the customer next to them, saying, "Lucy, can you do this order? It's the client's birthday in three days and they want it completed." Considering the turnaround is three days, I would have to stay there and finish it, and do extra work to get back on top of all my other work. I told her I had promised my husband that I'd go home, but she'd reply, "Aw, it's

their birthday, this is a $5000 sale, if you don't do this, she's not going to purchase."

'It felt like I had no control over my work or workload. I never felt like I could say no. No matter how much I tried to justify my feelings, it was as if they never had as much value as what the customer or my boss's needs were, they were never as important. I had no say.'

Lucy, professional

How can a lack of control be experienced?

- A lack of control over our schedules and time management.
- Having little or no influence over decision-making, or having accountability without power.
- A lack of say over *how* we do our work, with little or no input into how we can shape our job.
- A lack of opportunity to work using our strengths.

- A lack of flexibility or say in the scope or direction of our work (either day-to-day or longer term).
- A lack of control over our career path.
- Little or no access to the necessary resources to do our job.
- Constantly shifting priorities that we have no say over.
- Micromanagement, or an overly dictatorial management style by a direct manager.
- Lack of input into important decisions that affect our work.

This last factor, as well as having no say over how she and her colleagues were able to do their job, were contributing factors for Jenny.

'I think not being listened to was one of the causes of my burnout. Trying to build a relationship with the management structure, who you know you need to work alongside to change things, but them being so rigid and the process being so slow. And you're not actually invited to be a part of the process. No matter what you

say, very little changes for the good.'
— Jenny, surgeon

3. INSUFFICIENT REWARD

'I just didn't think that I was a person to them. It felt like "Oh, look. There's a bum on a seat. We'll just find another bum on the seat to do that."'
Annie, professional who experienced burnout

A third major contributor to burnout is insufficient reward. Now you might think this only has to do with money ('I'm not getting paid enough to do this!'), but financial reward is too simplistic and narrow a definition when we're referring to insufficient reward as a cause of burnout. Financial reward is what we call a 'hygiene factor'. What that means is that it's a 'maintenance issue' when it comes to motivation—it has to be present to avoid dissatisfaction. But it does not, in itself, provide satisfaction.

Reward has more to do with *balance*. It includes financial compensation, but it's not limited to that. Insufficient reward is an imbalance between how much we feel we invest in our job in comparison to how much we feel we are rewarded for that investment—something called distributive justice.

Reward includes both tangible and intangible benefits. It might mean recognition, respect or a simple thank you. It might relate to the reward of making progress—'Am I making headway towards the goals that are important to me?' It might be approval from those stakeholders within your organisation who matter to you—'Does my boss tell me when I'm doing a good job?', for instance.

And, of course, it *can* be financial—'Am I getting paid enough for what I do?'

'That's the hard part, that there's a constant pressure on you. And constant talk about how many surgeries you're behind in, how many appointments you're behind in. But I don't think it was once

said to me, "Thank you for doing a good job."'

Amanda, surgeon

In a nutshell, if we don't feel valued in a way that is important to us, this can not only lead to disengagement and lower productivity, it can also lead to burnout.

Combine a lack of reward with overwork and these causes quickly become intertwined. Often executives I have worked with say things like, 'I'm working my butt off and doing long hours, without the tools to do my job—and I'm not getting rewarded for it either!'

4. A SENSE OF ISOLATION

'People don't realise this, but medicine's actually lonely. You might be with people all day long, but because you work alone, by yourself usually (particularly in general-practice), you don't have anybody else to connect with on an ongoing basis. You might ask a second opinion, you might help

somebody else, but you don't sit very often and socialise. You don't do things together.'

Simon, medical professional

As well as wanting to have some control over our lives, we humans are hardwired for connection. We're tribal by nature. Our survival since time began has relied on us finding 'our people' and having a sense of belonging. In fact, social isolation can even affect the development of our brain's structure.

But, according to research, we're feeling more isolated and lonely now than ever. This is especially the case in Western societies. According to a 2020 Cigna study in the US, three out of every five adults, or 61 per cent, sometimes or always feel lonely. Among workers aged 18–22, 73 per cent of those studied reported sometimes or always feeling alone, up from 69 per cent in previous years. And according to that study, at work, men feel much more isolated than women.

We spend a significant proportion of our waking time at work. So it's no wonder that this loneliness can be felt in the workplace, as well as in our personal lives. This sense of isolation, or breakdown of a sense of community at work, is another major cause of burnout.

What causes a sense of isolation at work?

Isolation at work has many causes, both subtle and direct. Intentionally being ostracised by co-workers, or experiencing micro-aggressions due to race or gender, are just two examples of this.

However, any workplace or team that doesn't create psychological safety (a sense of team members feeling accepted and respected) or inclusion can also foster isolation. Psychological safety is not only important to counteract isolation, it's important for team performance, too. Research by Google, which conducted over 200 interviews with its employees, showed that psychological safety was one of the five key dynamics that set successful teams apart from other teams at Google.

Psychological safety and trust get eroded by workplace politics, and excessive or harmful workplace politics can play a role in burnout. For example, in the 2020 Cogo research, those saying that work politics get in the way of them doing a good job every day or a few times a week were far more likely to show signs of burnout. They were more likely to experience:
- exhaustion (87 per cent, compared to just 44 per cent of those who reported workplace politics getting in the way less regularly/never)
- isolation (55 per cent versus 12 per cent)
- depersonalisation (50 per cent versus 19 per cent)
- lack of engagement (83 per cent versus 39 per cent).

Common sources of a sense of isolation at work

- Ostracisation, micro-aggressions or bullying

- A workplace or team that does not provide psychological safety, or a sense of respect or inclusion
- Physical working environments (such as office layout and remote-working situations)
- An imbalance of age and experience
- Poor onboarding/induction or poor integration of new hires
- Cliquey work environment or workplace culture
- Individual behaviour or personality traits. Increasingly, scientists believe that you can be genetically predisposed to loneliness—you can be born with a higher tendency to this trait
- Burnout! Yes, that's right. Burnout can lead to people withdrawing, which in turns makes them feel more isolated
- Conflict in the workplace that is unhealthy or not well managed.

Perceived loneliness at work doesn't just lead to burnout—it also has implications for productivity and engagement.

Trust, openness and respect—each cornerstones of high-performing teams—become equally pivotal when looking at isolation and burnout.

'It felt like I had forced my way into a job where I wasn't wanted. I was also bringing a new skill to the hospital that was met with a lot of resistance.'

Jenny, surgeon

'To work in a team where you feel very alone also sucked, because you didn't feel supported and you felt like more of the load is on you.'

Lucy, professional

This is where a person's relationship with their direct manager is pivotal. There's a saying that people don't leave organisations, they leave their manager. A lack of support and communication with your direct manager can contribute to feelings of isolation. But if you have a supportive, trusting and connected relationship with your direct manager, it reduces isolation and acts as a powerful social-connection buffer to burnout.

According to a 2018 Gallup survey, employees who feel strongly supported by their manager are *70 per cent less likely* to experience burnout on a regular basis.

> *'Overall I believe the organisation that I work for appreciates their workers and is concerned about our mental wellbeing. But my immediate manager and even my state manager, although they say they are compassionate, that is really lip service and is not really carried out in their actions.'*
> Respondent, Cogo Workplace Wellbeing Survey

> *'At my workplace my direct manager is awesome. However, mental health and wellness is just a tick-box exercise by the CEO.'*
> Respondent, Cogo Workplace Wellbeing Survey

These responses show us that the organisation and the direct manager need to be in alignment when it comes to ensuring employees feel supported in their mental wellbeing. One without the other, while still positive, reduces the multiplied benefit and increased engagement the organisation could be getting from their employees.

5. AN ABSENCE OF FAIRNESS

'We're employed in what's called tenths, that's a half day, so five hours. So, I do nine tenths, and then we do our turn on call. Early on, we only had two registrars, so we were on call 50 per cent of the time with no registrar. When I was employed, there was no equity between who was working what, and who was working on what contract. So I see someone who's employed full time working a whole day less than I do! It's complete inequity.'

Jenny, surgeon

Humans are keenly attuned to the concept of fairness. In this context, fairness is the extent to which we perceive decisions at work as being fair and equitable. A lack of perceived fairness in the workplace contributes to burnout. Feeling that we are being treated unfairly—particularly when it relates to aspects such as promotion, inequity in workloads or inequalities in pay—can be a big contributor to burnout.

We might not always *like* what leaders within our organisation choose to do, but if the process and communication are perceived to be *fair*—and trust, openness and respect are deemed to be present—then burnout is far less likely to rear its ugly head.

Justice and fairness affect employee engagement, employee turnover and productivity. But justice and fairness have particularly strong implications when it comes to burnout. A longitudinal study of 1600 employees by Dutch psychologist Jan Fekke Ybema from Utrecht University in the Netherlands in 2008 showed that there is a direct correlation between injustice and burnout. In particular, those people who experienced 'distributive injustice' (which relates to inequity of one's own rewards or outcomes, such as salary and esteem, compared with that of colleagues) are more likely to develop burnout over time.

So, a perceived absence of fairness and justice leads to burnout—and not by a small amount. Employees who feel they're treated unfairly at work are 2.3 times more likely to experience a high level of burnout, according to Gallup.

Common examples of an absence of fairness at work

- Unfair treatment or being unfairly targeted
- Favouritism
- Unfairness when it comes to pay, perks or prestige
- Inequity in promotions, or being overlooked
- Communication—whether someone's voice gets heard in meetings far less than others
- Inequity in workloads

   'At the end of term, my three upper levels of management compounded an already stressful time by adding much more to our workload. The inequity of how it was done was awful ... There are

protected staff all through the organisation who have nowhere near the workload of others, which is so hard to watch whilst I am one of the most diligent and hard working.'
Respondent, Cogo Workplace Wellbeing Survey 2020

6. VALUES CONFLICT

A disconnect between an organisation's and employee's value set is our final driver of burnout, particularly if that gap persists and widens over time. As Michael Leiter and Christina Maslach put it, 'The greater the gap between individual and organisational values, the more often staff members find themselves making a trade-off between work they want to do and work they have to do. In some cases, people might feel constrained by the job to do things that are unethical and not in accord with their own values.'

Research has found that a conflict in values is related to all three dimensions of burnout—exhaustion, cynicism and professional inefficacy.

This was demonstrated to me starkly when I was in executive search. Christie was a senior executive whom I had known for most of her career. I had watched her climb the corporate ladder over the course of a decade with several different organisations. She was a high performer with a great track record, and previous employers waxed lyrical about her performance, passion and dedication. She had thrived in both large corporates and smaller organisations.

When she phoned me excitedly one day to let me know she had just taken a newly created COO role with a high-profile, family-owned, fast-moving consumer goods (FMCG) organisation, I was both excited and cautious. The owner and founder of this company was a successful entrepreneur, but with a very strong and unusual value set and business approach.

I kept my concerns to myself. Christie had already made her decision, and I didn't want to dampen her bubbling-over enthusiasm about her latest career move. I also was sure that Christie had done her due diligence on the culture and value set of her new employer; she was thorough like that.

I didn't hear from Christie for nine months. There were times when I thought to pick up the phone and check how the new job was going, but then I'd forget or the moment would pass. Then one day I received a short and unnaturally cautious email from Christie, wanting to catch up for a coffee. This didn't bode well.

When she walked into our offices, I was shocked. She had lost a heck of a lot of weight, had black rings under her eyes and her expression was one shrouded in defeat and anxiety. She was a shadow of her former self—hollow and burned out. This was not the Christie I had known.

For over an hour, through tears, Christie relayed how she had struggled in her new role. How she had been surprised, then worried at how different the owner's values were from her own. His value set (unsurprisingly) permeated every aspect of the company's culture and way of doing business. More and more, she felt forced to work at odds with her own values in order to fit in and succeed in his.

It wasn't that he was unethical or that there was anything wrong with his values per se. It was just that they were diametrically opposed to her own. Until then, she hadn't realised quite how important this values match was for her. Whereas one of her key values was inclusiveness, his was power and independence. Where he valued profit and shareholder value above other stakeholders, she valued employees and other stakeholders as being equally important as the shareholder.

The more Christie tried to emulate the founder and company's values, the more she felt she was abandoning her own. No wonder that in nine months she had become disconnected, burned out and was feeling alone. She was emotionally and physically exhausted. She even began to doubt her own worth and ability as a leader. And I saw a creeping cynicism in the way she spoke about the industry that she had previously loved so much.

By talking it through, Christie worked out that she was burned out—but not because of overwork. In other roles in other organisations, she had regularly worked longer hours. It was the values mismatch that was the big burnout lever here for her.

She began a planned exit from the organisation from that day. The happy ending to Christie's burnout story? She secured another role within four months—with a company whose value set was more in line with her own—and she regained all of her previous energy, performance and positivity.

KEY TAKEOUTS

- There are six main causes of burnout. They are overwork, a lack of control, insufficient rewards, a sense of isolation, the absence of fairness and a values conflict between the individual and the organisation or team.
- Any one of these causes can contribute to burnout, but when more than one is present, it's likely to increase the chances of burnout

occurring. There is an interconnectedness in these causes, and when they are intertwined, it creates a perfect burnout storm.

CHAPTER 6
WHAT WE CAN DO TO ADDRESS BURNOUT

'I am deeply concerned about the roll-out of [Employee Assistance Programme] /counselling/mindfulness/yoga/massage in workplaces. These (especially EAP/counselling) seem to be used as an alternative to acknowledging genuine issues that exist in workplaces. The MO is to somehow turn problems around to be the employees' fault and then say that the problem is with their mental health or "perspective". This is dangerous in my view and organisations should instead focus on addressing the root causes of the stressors, rather than fixing the symptoms.'

Respondent, Cogo Workplace Wellbeing Survey

Most organisations are waking up to the fact that they need to take care of their employees' *mental* wellbeing, as well as their *physical* wellbeing. But many are still grappling with exactly how to do this. We've seen a proliferation of yoga classes, mindfulness training and fruit bowls in the lunchroom. We've seen resilience courses and fitness programmes galore.

I don't want to diss these things. They all play their part. But burnout won't be fixed by a fruit bowl.

We need to do more than apply skin-deep solutions to, or stick reactionary Band-aids on, the issue of burnout. We must take a closer look under the bonnet of our organisations if we want to truly tackle burnout. We must examine the fabric of our organisations—our systems, priorities, organisational culture and our leadership practices. We need to ask ourselves, do these deeply embedded elements of our organisations support our people's mental wellness? Or do they contribute to mental distress and burnout?

It makes commercial sense to ensure that people, as well as profits, thrive. According to research by Ipsos MORI for Business in the Community in the UK, organisations that prioritise employee engagement and wellbeing outperform the average by approximately 10 per cent on the FTSE 100. And, as we've outlined earlier in the book, the costs of burnout to organisations are staggering. According to the World Economic Forum, the annual cost of burnout to the global economy is estimated to be £255 billion! Converted to New Zealand dollars that is over $500 billion, which is more than one-and-a-half times New Zealand's GDP.

Organisations without systems to support the wellbeing of their employees have higher turnover, lower productivity and higher healthcare costs, according to a report by the American Psychological Association (APA). Another study by the APA claims that burned-out employees are 2.6 times as likely to be actively seeking a different job, 63 per cent more likely to take a sick day and 23 per cent more likely to visit the emergency room.

Despite the benefits of tackling burnout in the workplace—and the costs of not doing so—organisations are still not doing enough. In many cases, it's not for lack of trying. It's my belief that most organisations are genuinely interested in supporting their people's wellbeing. It's just that, until now, we haven't yet quite got to the crux of *how*. We also often underestimate the power of simple solutions that are more difficult to get right organisation-wide—like leadership skills and behaviour. Rather, we think quick fixes or shallow symbols are the answer.

REDUCING TOP STRESSORS

We know that frequent, consistent stress is a precursor to burnout. So how can we reduce the top stressors? In the Cogo Workplace Wellbeing Survey 2020, respondents listed the following as contributing to the stress they felt at work:
- 'Work politics or bureaucracy' (selected by 46 per cent)
- 'The behaviour of manager/management' (30 per cent)

- 'An unrealistically high workload' (39 per cent)
- 'The way my work is scheduled/long hours' (24 per cent)
- 'Bullying and harassment and/or discrimination' (17 per cent).

These five stressors are ones that leaders and organisations can have a significant influence over. The 2020 Cogo survey also identified 'the nature of my work' as the top stressor, with 50 per cent of respondents selecting this. While this is not something that can always change, we *can* support people at work to cope better with this stressor by providing them with coping strategies to stop this stress leading to burnout.

The 2020 Cogo survey found a disconnect between what leaders in organisations are experiencing and think is working—and what their employees are experiencing. Of the owners/operators/C-level executives who were surveyed, 61 per cent agreed that their workplace did a good job at supporting mental and physical wellbeing. This compared with just 36 per cent of general staff.

So, when we look at adopting strategies for wellbeing, we need to ensure that what we're doing works for *all* staff, not just those at the top table. It's not enough to ask employees what's working or not working for them. We should also be actively seeking their ideas on what *will* work. Some organisations undertake staff surveys on wellbeing and engagement, but either don't involve employees in coming up with solutions or, worse, pay lip service or don't do much with the survey results.

Involving your teams in identifying possible solutions for what will affect them makes sense. It may take you longer to identify what to do, but you'll save time in the long run, as employees are more likely to buy in to the solutions and activities immediately, rather than waiting to see how things go—or, even worse, actively disagreeing with what management believes is the right thing to do.

THE IMPACT LEADERSHIP HAS ON BURNOUT

The impact of leadership on burnout is getting increasing attention from the scientific community—and with good reason. A number of studies have shown a direct link between unskilled and poor leadership practices and increased rates of burnout.

When you examine the causes of burnout, as we've done in the previous chapter, it's not a big leap to make the connection between leadership behaviour and resultant burnout in those they lead. How? The causes of burnout—overwork, lack of control, isolation, lack of reward and fairness, and a values mismatch—are all affected and influenced significantly by the leadership within an organisation.

Take Amanda, Lucy and Simon, for instance, who were professionals who experienced burnout. All cited a lack of support from management as a significant contributing factor to their burnout, combined with unrealistic expectations. As Amanda remarked, 'You start realising that there are so many things they [management] don't want to change—and that, at the end of the day, I felt like they're just going to throw me under the bus. If something happens, I didn't feel like they were going to support me as a person who's working for them.'

> *'The burnout trigger was just feeling a lack of support.'*
>
> Lucy

They also spoke of the unrealistic expectations of leaders that were placed on them:

> *'They kind of expect you to be a god, expect you to never get anything wrong...'*
>
> Simon

> *'I think the biggest issue [in terms of support and expectations] for doctors is that there is that pressure of being this wonder person, whether you're Wonder Woman or Superman...'*
>
> Amanda

Encouragingly, though, just as leadership behaviour and workplace culture can aggravate and cause burnout, it can also do the opposite. High levels of leader support have consistently been shown to reduce burnout.

The relationship we have with our direct manager packs a particularly big punch. Studies have shown that the leadership qualities of direct supervisors have a link to whether their direct reports suffer from burnout—or not.

The upshot? It's becoming pretty clear that *how* a leader leads has a fundamental influence on whether or not their team members suffer burnout. In other words, leadership has a significant impact on both the *prevention* and *cause* of burnout in employees.

WHAT CAN LEADERS DO?

If all this seems just a bit overwhelming to tackle if you're a leader, fear not. We can move beyond burnout.

In the coming chapters, we cover four key strategies for reducing burnout in the workplace, and explain why they're so effective. We also include practical tools to help individuals, leaders and organisations apply these four strategies and kick burnout to the curb.

I call these four strategies the four '-ises': Recognise, Destigmatise, Socialise and Organise.

RECOGNISE

We can take the first step by learning to *recognise* the signs of burnout. Burnout can creep up on people, so learning to pick up on the early warning signs is a crucial step towards reducing it in workplaces.

There are three red flags that leaders can look out for in themselves and in those they lead, that indicate that someone may be suffering from burnout. In the forthcoming chapter, 'Recognise', we outline these three red flags—the signs to look out for. We outline why burnout can be so difficult to spot, especially in the early stages.

There are different stages of burnout; a bit like a candle burning down, burnout doesn't happen overnight. Identifying the early-stage signs helps us all (especially leaders) reduce the chances of burnout going undetected until it has reached an extreme. (Appendix B will help you identify these stages.)

DESTIGMATISE

Destigmatising burnout in the workplace is another key step we need to take in tackling this serious issue. It's difficult to address a problem if it remains hidden.

Burnout, like most mental distress in the workplace, frequently remains concealed. In many workplaces, stigma and shame drive it underground. Many people experiencing burnout (let alone more stigma-laden mental distress) are too afraid to open up about their experience for fear of negative repercussions to their job, career or even connection with their colleagues.

This is where leaders in an organisation must play a vital role. Those with positional power pack a bigger punch when it comes to changing a culture. Therefore, leaders have more clout when it comes to destigmatising not only burnout, but also mental distress in general in our workplaces. That said, we can all play our part in this, whether we have a formal title of 'leader' or not.

The 'Destigmatise' chapter outlines specific practices that leaders at all levels within an organisation can take to destigmatise burnout. It also provides organisations, on a holistic level, with specific tools to employ that can dismantle the shroud of stigma that often cloaks burnout—thus making it psychologically safe for people to talk about it. And, because we all have influence, this chapter also provides us as individuals with things we can do to help destigmatise burnout in our workplaces.

SOCIALISE

As we've outlined in the 'Causes of burnout' chapter, one of the biggest contributors to burnout is a growing sense of isolation—either perceived or real. And there are many forces at play in today's workforces that are contributing to people feeling lonelier or more disconnected at work than ever before.

But, once again, leaders can have a significant impact on this if they're purposeful in creating conditions for social connection. This means consciously working on building a respectful and trusting relationship not only with each of their direct reports but also *between* team members.

Organisations can have a massive impact by looking at the culture and work practices that can encourage connection. In the 'Socialise' chapter, we explore why humans are hardwired for connection and why the benefits of building stronger social connections at work pays off. We also outline some practical ways that leaders and individuals, as well as organisations, can take positive steps, that are meaningful and effective to strengthen social connections.

ORGANISE

Finally, in the 'Organise' chapter, we take a closer look at a critical leadership and organisational practice that packs a big punch when it comes to stamping out burnout and negative stress in the workplace—that is, how leaders, organisations and individuals can organise and prioritise work better to stop burnout in its tracks.

We explore why organisational systems, culture and processes can influence burnout rates. We outline tips and tools such as delegation and simple prioritisation that can have massive positive effects—and how individuals can apply some of these practices on a micro level themselves, including how to better manage their workload.

We offer practical strategies for leaders to give employees clear and realistic goals, as well as the support and resources they need to meet those goals.

If you think these actions outlined above seem like common sense, you'd be right. However, as the saying goes, 'common sense ain't that common!' Gallup and other researchers have found that a surprising number of employees feel that their direct manager fails to provide guidance or support in one or all of these areas.

It's important to remember that even if you do not hold a formal position of leadership, *you can still do something to make things better when it comes to spotting, stopping and stamping out burnout.*

You don't have to hold a title of 'manager' or have direct reports to be a leader. Anyone in an organisation can take a leadership role and exact influence. Maybe you're an individual contributor in your company. Maybe you work for yourself. You can apply the four -ises personally or influence others higher up the food chain to do so, too. Although hierarchical power is alive and well in organisations, I've seen amazing acts of personal leadership by individuals without the official title of 'leader' which have led to tremendous positive change in their organisation. As anthropologist Margaret Mead said, 'Never doubt that a small group of thoughtful, committed citizens can change the world; indeed, it's the only thing that ever has.'

KEY TAKEOUTS

- If the vast research pointing to the growing issue of burnout in our workplaces seems overwhelming, fear not. There's a lot we can do to spot it, stop it and stamp it out, whether that's at an organisational, leadership or individual level.

- That said, leadership—good and bad—is perhaps the biggest lever of all when it comes to addressing burnout.
- There are four strategies that I have coined which address burnout. They are *recognise, destigmatise, socialise* and *organise.* These can be applied whether you're taking an organisational, leadership or individual lens. We cover these next.

CHAPTER 7

RECOGNISE

> *'Not knowing why is, itself, a profound type of suffering.'*
> Emily Nagoski, author of *Burnout: The Secret to Unlocking the Stress Cycle*

That morning I dropped Nicholas off to school, so emotionally depleted I couldn't even muster the energy to give him a hug, is a morning that will be etched in my mind forever.

For weeks afterwards, I was horrified, mainly with myself. How could I have missed the warning signs? How could I have let things get so bad that I couldn't connect on the most basic, maternal level with one of the most important people in my life?

I berated myself incessantly. If I'd just recognised the symptoms earlier, I would not have left my wee man on the footpath outside his school, wondering what he'd done to lose his mum's affection.

Hindsight's a bitch.

What I realise now is that my direct manager, Nick, and I were both remarkably ill-equipped to recognise, let alone address, my symptoms of burnout before I reached this state.

These days, I know a bit more about burnout. I know how it can creep up on people, and I am more familiar with the red flags that indicate someone is heading down the burnout road. This chapter will help you to spot the signs of burnout, too.

EXHAUSTED. DEPLETED. DEFLATED.

These are three words many people use to describe the feelings of burnout. But in many cases, it's not until those feelings are extreme that they recognise them as burnout and (sometimes) do something about it.

It doesn't help that many people suffering from burnout are reluctant to admit they're suffering from it at all.

The fear of negative recriminations—stigma, career limitation or being seen as mentally weak—is both real and common. As Simon, a physician who suffered from burnout, who we interviewed for this book, noted about many of his colleagues in the medical profession, 'They can't admit it to somebody else, because it means they're failures, that they're not doing their jobs properly.'

Most people suffering from burnout remain at work. In many cases, those sinking into the quicksand of burnout can't see their own predicament clearly. They don't see the insidious creep of exhaustion, cynicism and professional inadequacy for what they are—the three key red flags of burnout.

Jenny, who suffered from burnout, didn't see these signs, but her colleagues did.

> 'My colleagues knew that I wasn't right for a long time. I'd be in tears in the office, things would go wrong. Actually, four months before I went off [on leave for burnout] two of my colleagues said, "Do you think you need to take

> some leave?", and I said, "No, no, I'm fine, I'm fine!" I didn't identify it myself, but other people could see it.'

Recognising the signs of burnout—in yourself, in your teammates and in those you lead—is a critical step to preventing it.

But there's a catch.

Unless you know what you're looking for, burnout can be difficult to pinpoint, especially in the early stages. The signs can be subtle. In some cases, they can go undetected until they've become extreme, appearing apparently out of nowhere and hitting us in the face.

This was the case for Jenny. For her, her first realisation that something was wrong was when the burnout was so extreme it literally stopped her in her tracks. Here's her story:

> 'The first time I realised I was burned out or heading to that point was actually just when I flipped out. I was on call, I went to Zumba, and I always have my phone on so I can hear it, and I got a phone call to say that one of the other surgeons was having problems and

could I go in and help her? And I said, "Sure." And then I felt this overwhelming sense of absolute dread.

'Next, I got another phone call on top of the first one saying there was a two-year-old boy with a coin stuck in his oesophagus. Could I come in and sort that out? And all of a sudden, I just—my brain just went "Bzzzt!", and I thought, "I don't want to go anywhere, I don't want to do anything, I just want to go home."

'I came home and got changed and went to help the other surgeon. On the way in, I could barely keep the car on the road. When I got out of the car, I was shaking so badly, and it was just like—I couldn't even string two thoughts together. My brain was just firing everywhere. I got into the tearoom, and luckily, there were two surgeons in there who I'd worked with before. And they both took one look at me and said, "Are you all right?", and I said, "No, I don't know what's happened." So one of *the other surgeons called in another surgeon to take over my call, and I came home. And basically, I slept for four months.'*

Not only can they be difficult to spot, but the early symptoms of burnout can also be easy to misdiagnose—hyper-productivity, a reluctance to take holidays, over-conscientiousness, an 'always on' vigilance and an inability to switch off. In some cases, these symptoms are viewed positively in work cultures.

People can also display the symptoms of burnout differently. For example, as we touched on in our look at 'Who is most at risk of burnout?', research has shown that women have been shown to report feelings of exhaustion, whereas men are more likely to demonstrate cynicism. Two people doing the same job might react differently to the same stressors, or they may demonstrate different symptoms that each characterise burnout.

If you learn to recognise the signs of burnout—not just in yourself, but also in those you lead—you're more likely to nip it in the bud. You're also more likely to reduce its repercussions—for the person suffering, for you as their direct manager, for their colleagues and, ultimately, for the organisation.

THE DIFFERENT STAGES OF BURNOUT

Burnout is a slow burn. It doesn't happen overnight. You don't wake up one morning feeling engaged and energised and then, the very next day, feel burned out. Just like a candle melting, burnout tends to happen slowly.

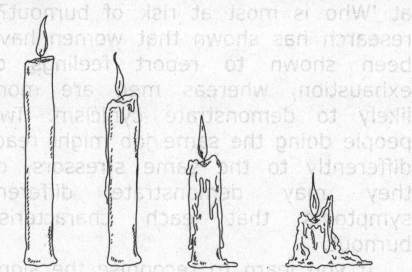

For a more in-depth look at the different stages of burnout, check out Appendix B. These stages are worth understanding, so that you can recognise the slippery slope. However, the most important thing when it comes to recognising burnout is to look out for the three major red flags. We'll take a look at those now...

THE THREE RED FLAGS OF BURNOUT

As we've touched on in previous chapters, there are three red flags (or symptoms) which indicate that burnout is in play. They are:
- chronic exhaustion,
- cynicism or depersonalisation, and
- a reduced sense of accomplishment or professional efficacy.

The 3 red flags of burnout

Someone suffering from burnout is likely to demonstrate a combination of signs that point to these three factors. These three dimensions, coined by Maslach and Leiter, are now the gold standard when it comes to diagnosing burnout and are widely recognised by researchers and practitioners alike.

Looking back on my own experience, it was clear these red flags were furiously flapping in my face—I just couldn't see them. And neither could Nick, my manager. I was in the vicious circle of burnout, but I didn't realise it.

If we had both been more aware of these red flags back then, we might have had a better chance of catching it earlier. So let's take a closer look now at each one of them, and how we can best recognise them, in more detail.

RED FLAG #1: CHRONIC EXHAUSTION

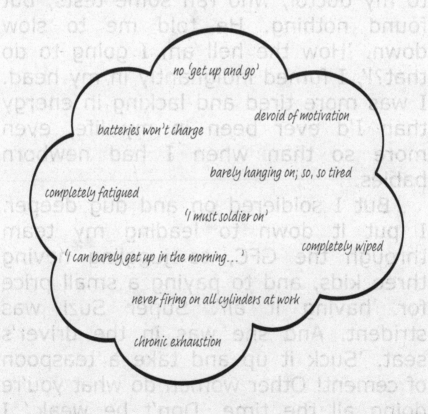

When I was burned out, my exhaustion was bone deep, chronic and all-consuming. I'd wake up exhausted (my baby girl was still waking in the night, but I was also suffering from bouts of insomnia over work), so I'd go to work exhausted. I'd come home exhausted. And I'd spend my weekends exhausted (trying to hide it and appear 'social' and happy for my husband and friends). I couldn't seem to get over this bone-deep tiredness. I even went to my doctor, who ran some tests, but found nothing. He told me to slow down. 'How the hell am I going to do that?!', I fumed indignantly in my head. I was more tired and lacking in energy than I'd ever been in my life, even more so than when I had newborn babies.

But I soldiered on and dug deeper. I put it down to leading my team through the GFC, to juggling having three kids, and to paying a small price for 'having it all'. Super Suzi was strident. And she was in the driver's seat. 'Suck it up and take a teaspoon of cement! Other women do what you're doing all the time. Don't be weak,' I told myself. But as I said these things inside my head, I wondered how I'd have enough energy to get through another day at work.

We've all experienced times at work when we're exhausted or 'over it'. Ebbs and flows in energy and motivation are part of working life. We can expect to have periods of intense activity and higher stress sometimes. It's natural for us to feel fatigued during these times. Even feeling weary at the end of a week, or at the conclusion of a big project, is not only likely—it's normal. But we take a break, we rest and our tank fills up again. We're then ready to face the next challenge with our batteries recharged.

That's not burnout.

Burnout is a chronic, debilitating and relentless exhaustion that's prolonged and—if left unchecked—extreme. It's when that holiday or the weekend off doesn't do its job. The exhaustion just won't go away. This tiredness is way more incapacitating than usual work-weariness. It can't be remedied by short breaks. It's when our batteries can't recharge, no matter how much we plug them into whatever normally recharges us.

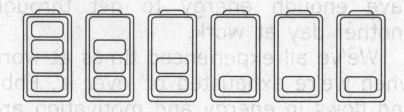

It's when our usual 'bounce back' factor doesn't ... well, bounce back.

Our bodies can be a litmus test. Ongoing physical and mental exhaustion can be markers of burnout. For Jenny, this presented as physical exhaustion:

'I remember my really good friend and mentor, who had known me from when I was a junior registrar, would try and take me out swimming to just try to give me a relief between home and work. But I just couldn't do it. I just had to get out of the pool. It

was too much. I couldn't enjoy it at all.'

SOME QUESTIONS WHICH MAY INDICATE BURNOUT-LEVEL EXHAUSTION:

- Do you feel physically exhausted or 'wiped out'?
- Do you feel tired all the time?
- Do you go on holiday or take a break but come back just as bushed?
- Do you always experience an overwhelming sense of relief that the weekend has finally arrived?
- Do you worry that there is no time you can take off work without negative consequences?
- Are you experiencing difficulty or an inability to concentrate at work?
- Do you feel as though you have nothing left to give?
- Do you drag yourself to work and have trouble getting started?
- Do you lack the energy to be consistently productive?

If you (or someone you lead) answers 'yes' to some or most of these questions, it could be a sign of burnout-level exhaustion.

Let's take a closer look at the second red flag...

RED FLAG #2: INCREASED CYNICISM AND DEPERSONALISATION

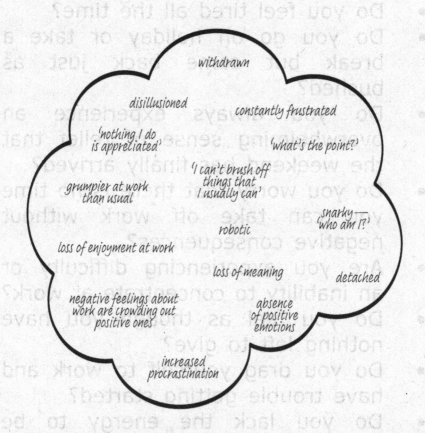

When I look back, I was also beginning to demonstrate the second red flag of burnout—cynicism and detachment. I have an at-times 'Pollyanna'-ish sense of enthusiasm. However, as I began to sink under the weight of exhaustion and inefficacy, with no end in sight, I found my usual 'glass-half-full' approach replaced by snarky cynicism. This cynicism was especially directed towards our US head office, whom I blamed for taking away my ability to have control over what we were doing in our New Zealand office. I even shot off a few (almost) career-limiting emails during this time to my boss's boss. Eek! A colleague later told me how weird it was to witness this 'Cynical Suzi'. It certainly wasn't the manager he knew.

If it was strange to witness, it was even stranger to experience. I began to withdraw and detach—even from family and friends.

People experiencing burnout find no joy where they once delighted in whatever work they were doing. This detachment forms the second key symptom of burnout—a prevalence of cynicism and depersonalisation (when you start to feel distant or have an indifferent attitude towards work). The burned-out person becomes increasingly cynical. And if their default approach was somewhat cynical to start with, they can become downright disparaging.

When a person is experiencing burnout, empathy drops and emotional distance rises. Pessimism, irritability and mistrust abound. And they can infiltrate all aspects of that person's professional life. It can even show up as bitterness, directed towards colleagues, customers or clients or patients, the organisation itself—or, perhaps most destructively, towards themselves.

This cynicism and depersonalisation can have particularly significant implications for those who do 'people-focused' work or those in the 'helping professions' which we outlined in the 'Who is most at risk?' chapter. Medical professionals, social workers, teachers, firefighters, paramedics and police all fall into this camp, as caring for others is central to their role.

'I mean, I'm not a really grumpy person. But I was getting

> *grumpier and grumpier. I don't know—you're just kind of not yourself.'*
>
> Amanda

Cynicism packs a big punch when it impacts not only those who are suffering, but also those people the burned-out person is interacting with. A burned-out teacher with increased cynicism may connect less with the children she teaches. The burned-out police officer with increased cynicism is more likely to act with less empathy or emotional regulation with the public. And physician burnout has been linked to compromised patient safety, unprofessionalism and lower patient satisfaction. Take Jenny again:

> *'I really withdrew from any meaningful relationships with colleagues. I couldn't even listen to people in a room talk about problems, I didn't want to bloody know about it. I couldn't deal with it ... I really felt like I wasn't doing anything. Ward rounds were far less enjoyable; it was just that I felt I couldn't connect with patients at all.*

> *And usually I'm quite a friendly person, and I just didn't want to extend that friendship aspect.'*

It doesn't take a rocket scientist to see that cynicism in the workforce is a dangerous and contagious virus that spreads throughout teams and organisations. With the backdrop of engagement in organisations across the globe being at an all-time low—something that every HR professional and CEO alike is wringing their hands about—cynicism is like adding fuel to the low-engagement fire.

One burned-out executive leading the New Zealand division of a global organisation, who I coached, admitted:

> *'I wondered who I'd become. I'm normally such a positive, "glass-half-full", "we-can-make-this-work" person. But after 18 months of dealing with constant restructuring, reduced resources and control over how I ran the local operation, I became extraordinarily cynical. Headcount cuts, combined with increased delivery expectations, the third restructure in 12 months and a constantly changing strategic*

direction from global Head Office was too much, even for me, let alone my team. I heard myself say to my team one day, when a new edict from Head Office came through, "Why even bother doing this? It'll just change in a couple of months anyway." I was appalled. This cynical language and negative attitude was something that made me really sit up and take note. I didn't recognise myself. I was disparaging and cynical as hell.'

Resentment and cynicism are two sides of the same coin. People suffering burnout who we interviewed for this book spoke of this link and how resentment was an unwelcome and often surprising visitor that accompanied cynicism, which they had not experienced previously in their professional lives. As Lucy commented,

'Once resentment kicks in, it becomes a game of the last straw, but the last straw happened many times before I had the guts to quit. Burnout is a catalyst for realising that you don't love something quite as much as you thought you did.

Because I can guarantee that I've worked harder than I worked then, and not felt burned out, 100 per cent. But how I felt about my work at the time of experiencing burnout was different. Resentment is such a big thing. Resentment is the road to divorce from your work.'

SOME QUESTIONS WHICH MAY INDICATE BURNOUT-LEVEL CYNICISM AND DEPERSONALISATION:

- Have you developed a negative attitude towards your job, your colleagues or clients/service recipients/patients that wasn't there before?
- Are you noticing a withdrawal from your job and its associated problems or challenges?
- Do you frequently feel disillusioned about your job?
- Have you become cynical or critical at work?

- Are you experiencing a lack of recognition or not feeling rewarded for good work recently?
- Are you quicker to anger, more irritable or do you have less patience with those you work with than usual? Are you overreacting to minor nuisances?
- Are you calling in sick or looking for excuses to get out of work on a regular basis (behaviour which is 'not like you')?
- Do you find yourself avoiding social events (particularly work-related ones) that you once looked forward to?
- Do you have less patience, empathy and enthusiasm than normal?
- Have others commented that you seem careless in your relationship to your clients/service recipients/patients?
- Do you overall feel frustrated because of your work?
- Have you lost your enthusiasm for the job?

RED FLAG #3: REDUCED PERSONAL ACCOMPLISHMENT AND A LACK OF PROFESSIONAL SELF-EFFICACY

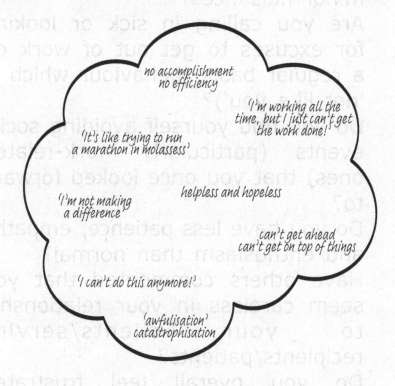

Perhaps my biggest sign of burnout was a growing sense of not achieving anything much at all at work. I was in quicksand, sinking lower and lower into a smothering pit of inefficacy. Suddenly, for the first time in my professional life,

I felt as if I didn't have the necessary resources or ability to do what was required of me.

I'd been an achiever my whole career. I was used to being on top. But I was not on top now. My performance was slipping away as quickly as my enthusiasm. I came to dread the weekly phone calls with Nick, my manager, which I had previously looked forward to with enthusiasm.

Burnout brings with it an increasing feeling of not accomplishing anything worthwhile at work. As you can imagine, this can be pretty soul-destroying, especially if you're used to achieving or you're passionate about the work you do.

When people who are suffering from burnout start to show this third symptom, and feel that it's increasingly difficult to accomplish what they're supposed to at work, it can be crippling.

There's an increasing feeling of not getting ahead or making headway, or that the work is becoming overwhelming and too challenging—even when previously this wasn't the case. A feeling that you're no longer having an impact is one of the most damaging signs of burnout, especially when you consider that one of the key motivators people strive for at work is making a difference.

It's no surprise that this can be a self-fulfilling prophecy. A sense of reduced personal accomplishment can be incredibly demotivating. This demotivation then leads to no enthusiasm and a loss of will to do the job. And yes, that self-fulfilling prophecy comes full circle—voilà, poor performance.

When I was in the midst of burnout, I won a big account for our firm. Usually, this would have had me dancing around our office and feeling proud of my accomplishment. But instead of feeling excitement and professional pride, I felt an overwhelming sense of dread about how I was going to deliver this project. I didn't feel like my team or I could do what was needed for this new key account we'd just landed. This major new client was a ten-kilo bag of cement slung around my shoulders when I was already knee-deep in mud, just trying to get to the finish line.

This reduced professional efficacy also came through in those people I interviewed for this book. For instance, Jenny noted:

> 'My brain was just constantly worried about what was going to happen next and how I was going to get all of those things done. And I was very inefficient, I think, because of that. If I had been worried at any point about patient safety I would've stopped. But I wasn't getting the same sense of satisfaction about what I was doing. I never felt I was good enough, but I didn't feel bad enough to not be doing it.'

SOME QUESTIONS WHICH MAY INDICATE A BURNOUT-LEVEL REDUCED SENSE OF PROFESSIONAL

ACCOMPLISHMENT AND LACK OF SELF-EFFICACY:

- Are phrases like 'nothing I do matters' or 'everything I do is wrong' or 'I can't do this' starting to pepper your speech? This is especially worth taking note of when you have previously had self-confidence and a sense of self-efficacy in your work.
- Do you feel that the demands of your job are unclear or unreasonable?
- Is work either no longer challenging, or has it become overwhelmingly challenging?
- Does your work seem chaotic or too high pressured?
- Is there a sense that there is no time you can take off work without negative consequences?
- Do you regularly feel like you have to be too many things for far too many people at work?
- Is your sense of being able to solve problems or achieve at work reducing?

- Are you increasingly feeling inadequate in your role?

WHAT TO DO BEFORE BURNOUT TAKES HOLD

Here's the good news when it comes to the *recognise* strategy: when we start to recognise the red flags, there are—encouragingly—things that we can do to prevent or reduce burnout before it takes hold.

Here are some of the things that individuals, leaders and organisations can do to better recognise burnout:

WHAT INDIVIDUALS CAN DO TO RECOGNISE BURNOUT

- **Educate yourself on the signs we've outlined in this chapter and the stages of burnout in Appendix B.** If you're starting to recognise these in yourself, this is your cue to take a pause and reflect on what's going on. Don't be like me and many of those who I interviewed for the book, who soldiered on thinking they could work through this if they just worked harder or ignored the warning signs. Ask yourself: who can I share what I'm experiencing with? A GP is an obvious confidential and professionally trained choice if speaking to your boss or HR representative is not an option as a first 'reach out'.

- **If you recognise these burnout signs in a colleague, reach out to them.** Don't leave them hanging! Check it out gently. Do what you can to lower any feelings of isolation they may be experiencing in feeling burned out. Like the story of Jenny in this chapter, colleagues can often spot burnout before the burned-out person does. Meaningful connection is a powerful antidote to burnout. A simple 'How are you?', followed by active listening, may help your colleague. You could mention the signs of burnout outlined in this chapter. With a compassionate approach, offering to

support them in any way you can will make a big difference.
- **Leave this book lying around** in the lunchroom or in the office and share it widely, especially with your boss.

WHAT LEADERS CAN DO TO RECOGNISE BURNOUT

- **Be aware of the signs of burnout** as laid out in this chapter—not only in yourself, but also in your peers and those you lead. Look for instances or patterns in your team of increased exhaustion, absenteeism, increasing frustration or cynicism and/or reduced personal inefficacy. Connect the dots. Use some of the checklists in this chapter and in the appendices to help you do this.
- **Talk openly with your team about the signs of burnout in a way that is supportive and non-judgemental.** Let your team know that if they recognise these signs in themselves or each other, you want to know. Most

importantly, ensure too that they know that you are there to support them, not judge.

- **Bring mental wellness conversations into your one-on-ones.** Ask, 'On a scale of 1–10, where 1 is terrible and 10 is awesome, how would you rate your wellness (including mental wellness) right now?' If it's low, explore (in a supportive way) what might be going on. Have a coaching conversation with them about recognising the signs of burnout (check out the appendices for useful coaching questions—).

- **Use this book as a starting point for conversations on this topic.** Share this book, and articles on stress and wellness in the workplace, with your team, and ask them to share their responses. Be courageous—haveyou ever experienced these symptoms? Ask, 'What could we do better as an organisation or within this team to more effectively recognise burnout?' Be open to whatever feedback you get. Listen actively and make it safe for your people to venture their views. Seek their feedback and ideas on how you can recognise signs of burnout and unsustainable, chronic stress within the team.

WHAT ORGANISATIONS CAN DO TO RECOGNISE BURNOUT

- **Develop a leader's guide with detailed information and resources** to help your leaders better recognise the signs and symptoms of burnout and high, unmanageable stress—not only for themselves, but also in those they lead. Provide this as part of your induction and training of your leaders throughout your organisation. This could also be included in your leadership, safety or wellness programmes. Occupational health and safety doesn't stop with walking between the green lines. It should extend to mental health and wellbeing too.

- **Incorporate specific wellness questions into your people-practices** that may highlight these burnout symptoms; in one-on-ones, culture surveys and team meetings. Integrating mental-wellness checkpoints into your operating rhythms can help you spot systemic and individual cases of burnout.
- **Start at the top—at CEO and executive-leadership-team level.** Discuss the signs and symptoms of burnout at the leadership-team level. You need to model what you want to see in your organisation, and this includes recognising the signs of burnout within your leadership team. Once again, make it safe for people to admit it if they suspect they're suffering from burnout, and don't make it career-limiting if they do.
- **Consider using the Maslach Burnout Inventory survey (see Appendix L) across your organisation,** particularly if you are in a high-risk profession or industry.

- **Order more copies of this book** and distribute it widely to your leaders.

> ## KEY TAKEOUTS
> - Recognising the symptoms of burnout is a key step to addressing it and preventing it from taking hold.
> - There are three red flags of burnout:
>   * extreme exhaustion
>   * cynicism or depersonalisation
>   * reduced personal efficacy.
> - Recognising these three red flags, especially when all three are present, is helpful when it comes to recognising burnout.
> - Burnout doesn't happen overnight—it's a gradual process. The four key stages of burnout are outlined in Appendix B, which can help you spot that you, or someone in your organisation, might be on the road towards burnout.

Now that we've covered the first strategy for tackling burnout—recognising it—let's take a look at the second strategy: destigmatising it.

CHAPTER 8

DESTIGMATISE

> '*Shame never drives positive behaviour.*'
> Brené Brown

> '*I believe there are more people who are struggling than will ever admit [it].*'
> Respondent, Cogo Workplace Wellbeing Survey 2020

> '*If your workplace asks you for honesty around stress and mental health, my experience is in the end, it is also used against you.*'
> Respondent, Cogo Workplace Wellbeing Survey 2020

We cannot bring attention to a problem if that 'problem' remains hidden. Likewise, we can't solve a problem if we cannot see it clearly.

Burnout thrives on silence.

Most people don't feel comfortable talking about their mental health at work. In fact, in one major study that looked at mental health in the workplace, almost 60 per cent of employees said they had never spoken to *anyone* at work about their mental-health status. Of those who had, just over half said it was either a neutral or negative experience. Hardly the sort of response that encourages us to speak up and be vulnerable at work about such a sensitive, yet critical, topic!

As Simon, a doctor, pointed out, when referring to stressful situations like patient complaints, 'Your colleagues don't talk about their cases, so you're all left thinking that you're the only one it's happened to. And that's a big thing.'

Like most mental distress in the workplace, burnout is shrouded in shame and stigma. This stops people not only from admitting they're suffering from it, but also from asking for help. In fact, many people experiencing extreme burnout will continue to soldier on. They're too scared to be open about their situation for fear of negative repercussions. As an executive coach, I've worked with leaders demonstrating symptoms of burnout who try to push through it, afraid that if they admit they're not coping, they might be seen as weak or a non-performer.

And yet the stories and statistics about the stigma surrounding burnout are set against a backdrop of eye-watering costs. As I've pointed out in Chapter 1, mental distress costs companies billions each year globally. Although some mental illnesses are not related directly to the workplace, *burnout* most definitely *is*. It sits squarely in the occupational realm. This is a key reason why reducing the stigma surrounding burnout (and other mental distress) must become a priority if we want to reduce its significant human and financial costs.

If we're to stamp out burnout in our workplaces, then destigmatising it is a vital step in the right direction. How we talk about burnout and mental health in our organisations has a significant bearing on its consequences. It also determines whether we alleviate suffering or make it worse.

Leaders have a particularly powerful role to play in doing this. Many leaders underestimate the shadow they cast; they don't realise that their whisper comes out as a shout. Take Linda Hudson, the president of the land and armaments group for US military contractor BAE Systems, as an example of this 'leader shadow' effect.

Hudson was the first female president of the General Dynamics Corporation, and found that when she tied her scarf a certain way, her female staff copied the look. She said in the *New York Times*:

> *'And that's when I realised that life was never going to be the way it had been before, that people were watching everything I did. And it wasn't just going to be about how I dressed. It was about my behavior, the example I set, the tone I set, the way I carried myself, how confident I was—all those kinds of things.'*

The upside of this phenomenon is that leaders can have a powerfully positive impact when it comes to destigmatising mental distress and burnout in our places of work. It's time for leaders and organisations to bring burnout out of the darkness of stigma and into the light of non-judgement in a way that does not shame or blame.

For the purposes of this chapter, I'll speak a lot more about the broader concepts of mental health and mental illness (or, my preferred term, mental distress). This is because although we're talking about burnout specifically, the importance of destigmatising mental distress encompasses the broader umbrella of mental health issues, not just burnout.

THE PROBLEM WITH SHAME

When I experienced burnout, I was filled with shame about it. I fell prey to one of the most common myths that surrounds burnout: that I was totally to blame. I believed that my burnout was completely my fault, and that I was mentally weak.

At that time, in our workplace there was no formal communication, resources or open discussion about mental distress. No leaders within our organisation spoke of their own struggles with stress. This had the effect of keeping me schtum about mine. It made me feel like I was the only one experiencing it.

Brené Brown, a US researcher on shame and author of *Dare to Lead*, wrote in an article for *Forbes* magazine entitled '3 Ways to Kill Your Company's Idea-Stifling Shame Culture',

'Make no mistake: humanising work requires courage. Honest conversations about vulnerability and shame are disruptive. The reason that we're not having these conversations in our organisations is that they shine light in the dark corners. Once there is language, awareness, and understanding, turning back is almost impossible.'

For many of us, our job is of central importance to our identity and self-worth. For some of us, it's paramount. Accomplishment and performance at work play a critical role in how many of us define ourselves. When we fall short, it feels shameful.

At the very least, work is where we spend the majority of our time, so it has the potential to have a substantial impact on our wellbeing. Burnout eats away at this identity, at our self-efficacy, our belief in ourselves—and that, in turn, leads to shame.

If you're suffering from burnout, you not only experience a myriad of physical and cognitive symptoms, you also experience emotional distress. The stereotypes, prejudice and discrimination related to burnout in the workplace just add to the burden.

What's worse is that the relationship between burnout and shame can be a circular one: burnout can lead to feelings of shame at work. And I believe that shame at work exacerbates symptoms of burnout, such as depersonalisation and reduced self-efficacy. It may also lead us to feel more isolated, which we also know is a cause of burnout.

The relationship between burnout & shame is a circular one

SOME SCARY STATISTICS ON SHAME AND BURNOUT

Here are some startling figures that show how reluctant people are to admit they are suffering from burnout:
- The World Health Organization (WHO) considers stigma to be one of the greatest barriers to the treatment of mental health challenges.
- The Cogo Workplace Wellbeing Survey 2020 of over 1500 New Zealanders and Australians showed that burnout symptoms such as levels of exhaustion and isolation were lower for those who:

—could talk to someone in a leadership/official HR position
  —believed their direct manager genuinely cared
  —could be open about stress and mental wellbeing without fear of negative consequences.
- In the 2019 New Zealand College of Law Performance and Well-Being Study, only 27 per cent of respondents said they would speak to senior staff or a manager to relieve stress.
- In another study, of surgical residents, stigma was identified as one of the top three barriers to seeking care for burnout. Ninety per cent of the residents and 78 per cent of attending doctors identified stigma, an inability to take time off to seek treatment, and avoidance or denial of the problem as their three biggest barriers to speaking out.
- Findings in a further three studies indicated that burnout was stigmatised at only a slightly lower level than depression, although other findings indicate that burnout

may *not* be less stigmatised than depression.
- Because companies are not doing enough to break down this stigma, many people don't self-identify as having a diagnosable mental-health condition, even though *up to* 80 *per cent* of us will experience one in our lifetimes.
- Burnout can be contagious. As burnout researchers have pointed out, burnout carries stigma while also being socially contagious. As burnout manifests in both our behavioural and social symptoms, our colleagues can pick up on some of the symptoms. 'This may then result in a double-edged problem: burnout prevalence grows (as the likelihood of self-labelling increases), while the likelihood of help-seeking behaviours decreases (thus preventing appropriate treatment).'

In some professions, workplace processes and rules exacerbate the problem of stigma, discouraging people from self-reporting burnout or mental illness. For example, in many countries, including New Zealand and Australia, medical professionals are required to disclose their mental-health history on professional applications such as for their annual practising certificate. This process is important, with very sound reasons behind it. But many medical practitioners are fearful of what it might lead to. For Simon, it felt as if he could not ask for support for fear of negative repercussions to his medical career.

> *'I felt like I couldn't get help because when I went to the Medical Council, if they asked me if I'd have any mental health records, I'd have to say "yes"—and I'd have to stand down or whatever.'*

HOW DO WE DESTIGMATISE BURNOUT?

Mostly, destigmatising burnout begins and ends with leadership. This means leadership at a macro level, as well as at a micro level.

At a macro level, leaders (in particular, senior leaders within organisations) can take a close look at their organisation's processes, culture and overall approach to mental wellbeing at work, including burnout.

At a micro level, individuals at *all* levels within an organisation can show leadership by playing a role in destigmatising burnout in their workplace. Something as simple as people speaking openly about burnout and mental health can significantly reduce the stigma. Even better? When leaders speak openly about their *own* mental-health journeys.

So let's take a look at what organisations, leaders and individuals can do to destigmatise burnout. I've deliberately started with what organisations and leaders can do, before turning our attention to what individuals can do to destigmatise burnout. That's because leaders and organisations can have the biggest influence on this strategy.

WHAT ORGANISATIONS CAN DO TO DESTIGMATISE BURNOUT

Despite the fact that experts tell us that one in four adults will struggle with a mental-health issue during his or her lifetime, in many organisational cultures we have a long way to go to normalise mental distress. It remains the realm of the 'other', even when it is so much a 'we' experience.

The prevailing culture of an organisation plays a crucial role in whether people are willing to admit they're suffering from burnout, or from any other mental distress for that matter. If yours is a culture that directly or indirectly insinuates that burnout is a sign of weakness, it will continue to be pushed underground.

Burnout isn't just the realm of HR, either. It's a business issue and one that is increasingly becoming a diversity, equity and inclusion issue, too.

Creating a workplace where people's mental wellness is a priority should be tackled at the highest levels within an organisation, particularly if yours is a profession which features prominently in the burnout statistics. This means that if you're a board member, a CEO or a senior executive (even if you're not responsible for HR), it's up to you to ensure that mental wellness of your people is on the strategic agenda—and that destigmatising burnout and mental distress is a priority as part of this.

There *are* some good news stories about. In a BBC article, 'Stress: Is it surprising bosses are stricken?' we see one such example.

John Binns was a partner for 10 years at accounting and consulting firm Deloitte. When he was signed off work in 2007 with depression, he thought it was the end of his career.

However, the opposite happened. He was told he was a valued member of the team and was supported to get back to work.

Following his return, he set up a mental-health champion scheme where employees could speak to any one of eight partners who had been trained in mental-health issues, outside of line management and HR. The scheme has been well reviewed and has been adopted by other organisations.

The encouraging point from this story is that Binns and his company were proactive, and started the journey to destigmatising mental distress in their workplace.

Making it easier for people to talk about their mental wellness, including stress and burnout, has some pretty big wins—not only for the employee, but also for the organisation. In Cogo's Workplace Wellbeing Survey 2020, those who were able to be open about the stress that they experience at work were less likely to:
- show signs of exhaustion (45 per cent versus 61 per cent for the whole sample)
- show signs of isolation (13 per cent versus 30 per cent)
- show signs of depersonalisation (21 per cent versus 32 per cent)
- show signs of low engagement (33 per cent versus 57per cent)
- take leave because of stress (19 per cent versus 34 per cent)

- experience bullying/harassment and/or discrimination (4 per cent versus 17 per cent)
- experience frequent stress—more than once a week (37 per cent versus 56 per cent). They were also more likely to feel like they could cope with the stress they did experience (64 per cent versus 48 per cent), despite the same percentage saying that the nature of their work was stressful.

These figures are compelling, and point to the tangible difference that being able to be open about mental distress makes. We need to make it OK for people to own up about the workplace stress they are experiencing. Actually, I would say we need to make it *more than OK*. We need to encourage and hold it up as a positive thing.

So, what specific things can we do to aid in this?

- **Start at the top.** It bears repeating: *burnout is not an HR issue.* It's one that should be sponsored, modelled and driven at CEO and board level, *supported* by HR. Given the implications of burnout, particularly in those professions and industries where it's especially prevalent, the CEO should take the lead in destigmatising burnout and mental distress in general. As Kelly Greenwood, Vivek Bapat and Mike Maughan tell us in their *Harvard Business Review* article, 'People Want Their Employers to Talk About Mental Health', 'CEOs can no longer afford to ignore it. Instead, they should serve as the normalizers-in-chief of mental health challenges'.

- **It is the bare minimum to ensure that you have adequate workplace counselling services that are both widely known and easily accessible in your organisation.** But given many services like these aren't accessed as much as they could be, merely having them available is not enough. You have to regularly communicate (again from the top) about their value. One high-performing and fairly blokey CEO I spoke to talked openly in his organisation about how he had used the EAP (Employee Assistance Programme) himself. This had the effect of making others in his company feel it was an OK thing to access and use as well. Ask yourself, are you regularly and vocally communicating about these mental wellbeing services and encouraging your employees to use them too? Are they easily and equally accessible to *all* your staff? If these services aren't working or being accessed, are you asking your employees for ideas on ways to make these services more useful? This quote from a respondent of the Cogo Workplace Wellbeing Survey further illustrates this point: 'Just because services are "offered" does not automatically make the workplace more caring or understanding about wellness, because they are not actually being proactive and targeting individuals.'

- **Incorporate a standard process to offer a session with a counsellor, or some similar service, at key points that have been identified in your industry**

or business as causing high stress.** For example, when a patient complaint is made to a doctor, after a particularly stressful or long-term project, or when someone is returning to work after parental leave.
- **Do a burnout and mental wellness audit across your organisation's systems and processes**—everything from recruitment and induction through to monthly one-on-ones. Is mental wellbeing featured in your operating rhythms?
- **Talk openly in organisational documents about mental wellbeing**—and not just in the wellness sections. Ensure that your intranet and your communication to your employees has mental wellness front and centre. Go one step further and have a section in your policies specifically on burnout, with a questionnaire outlining the signs and symptoms.
- **Report on mental wellbeing and burnout in your organisation.** As the adage goes, 'we respect what

we inspect.' Whether in your employee engagement survey, or by running a specific wellbeing or burnout survey such as the Maslach Burnout Inventory, measure mental wellness across your organisation. In measuring mental wellbeing, make sure that you're looking at specific indicators for measuring burnout. The resources listed in Appendix L can help organisations with this.

- **Ask your employees what they need** to be supported when it comes to stress and mental wellness.
- **Develop a leader's guide with detailed information and resources** to help them better destigmatise burnout and mental distress. Provide this as part of your induction and training of your leaders.
- Also, it's worth noting that **workplaces in New Zealand have a legal responsibility to manage risks to mental wellbeing and mental health,** just like they do any other health and safety risk.

This includes making sure there's no discrimination, and taking steps to reduce work stress to prevent psychological harm. This might surprise you—mental wellness is not usually given the same airtime or consideration as watching out for hazards or OT assessments of ergonomic workstations, for example—but it matters all the same!

WHAT LEADERS CAN DO TO DESTIGMATISE BURNOUT

If you're a leader and have personally suffered from burnout (or any other mental distress, for that matter), have the courage to share your story and talk about it—what it was like, what helped you get through it and heal, for example. Be open and vulnerable about your own mental-health challenges. Yes, this takes courage. But if others lower down in the organisational hierarchy can see that it's OK to be open, they're more likely to be open about it themselves (and, more importantly, with you as their manager) and to seek help. The more senior you are in your organisation, the more impactful this will be.

There are increasing numbers of high-profile and successful CEOs coming out publicly about their struggles with mental distress. This is a good thing. It normalises it and helps to break down the stigma. Any person with positional power can do this and it will have a positive impact.

For example, when Xero's chief executive Craig Hudson came out publicly about his battle with mental-health issues, here was the head of a highly successful company speaking openly about the need to talk more about mental health in the workplace. It made for a powerful juxtaposition between power and vulnerability. And in New Zealand, where rugby is the Holy Grail, Sir John Kirwan's admission of depression and his subsequent work in this space (including co-founding Mentemia) has had a huge impact, especially for men.

It is, of course, easier for some individuals than others to speak openly about those times in their life where they experienced issues with their mental wellbeing and the corresponding impacts. However, don't underestimate the power of a senior leader, who doesn't normally talk about their own life issues, sharing with their people those times when things weren't so rosy. This can be a significant step in bringing burnout and mental distress into the light as topics that can be talked about. In discussing them, it's also possible to see that you might be able to do something about them.

There is some good news emerging from the 2020 Cogo research about leaders speaking more openly about stress and mental wellbeing: senior staff are more likely to be open about the stress they experience at work compared with general staff (60 per cent of senior staff versus just 36 per cent of general staff). Let's keep this trend going. It makes a positive difference when it comes to destigmatising burnout and mental distress in our workplace—and in our society.

As well as sharing your own experiences, as a leader you can:

- **Share stories of other people who are well regarded within your industry who have struggled with burnout, received help and resumed successful careers.** When people see that burnout can be successfully overcome, it provides hope.
- **Start to share the idea that mental illness is a part of normal life,** as paradoxical as that may sound. The latest ground-breaking research published in *Scientific American* shows that you're more likely to experience a bout of mental illness in your life than you are to suffer diabetes, heart disease or cancer! Many of us would not self-identify with these statistics, despite the reality that up to 80 per cent of us will experience a diagnosable mental illness in our lifetimes.
- **Remember that every one of us is touched by mental illness.** It might not be us, but it will be a loved one—a family member, a friend, a colleague. So breaking down models of mental distress

being 'other' will help people recognise that this is an 'us' not 'them' issue.
- **Start to have more conversations about stress and burnout, informally as well as formally.** You can do this with your team as a whole and also in one-on-ones with your direct reports. One way to do this might be to start your one-on-ones by asking your direct report about their wellbeing. One government department I work with, for example, includes a wellbeing question at the beginning of its monthly operating reports (monthly one-on-ones with direct reports), whereby the employee rates their wellbeing and this opens up discussions with their manager on their mental wellbeing.
- **It's not just in one-on-ones that leaders can do this.** For team check-ins, leaders can start by asking about people's wellbeing or asking the team for a quick 'what's on top of your mind or taking up your headspace?'. When instigating

a team check-in, it's important to make sure everyone gets the chance to respond, not just some. Talking about it as a group takes the pressure off any one person. Ways to ask about mental wellbeing could include:

—How are you this morning? What's taking up your headspace today?

—On a scale of 1 to 10, how is everyone's wellbeing?

—How are you feeling today?

—Let's each share a highlight and a challenge we're facing right now ... I'll go first...

- **Create the psychological safety required for people to be open if they're struggling.** You can do this by explicitly encouraging everyone to speak up when feeling overwhelmed or starting to show the signs of burnout. When they do, don't shame or punish them but, rather, offer your help and support—through your actions and your behaviour. Merely listening with your full attention is a simple yet powerful way to do this.

- **Share an article about burnout with your team and have a conversation about it in your team meeting.** What stood out about the article you shared? Where would your team rate this organisation or this team on the causes of burnout? What steps could we take to safeguard this team from chronic stress and burnout? Having safe conversations about mental health is paramount to creating a culture of psychological safety. Psychological safety builds trust, and trust builds high-performing teams.
- **Get clear on, and publicise, ways for your people to get help.** In the Deloitte workplace survey we mentioned previously, nearly 70 per cent of respondents said that their employers were not doing enough to prevent or alleviate burnout. 'Bosses need to do a better job of helping their employees connect to resources before stress leads to more serious problems.' Resources, programmes, information, support—these are things that

employees should know about and be able to access easily and in a confidential manner.
- **Practise empathy. Improve your listening skills.** Leaders who are great listeners are not only perceived better, but listening is also a powerful way to demonstrate empathy. This can be as simple as asking the question, 'How are you?' (and then practising active listening when your employee responds). It could be saying in language that is right for you and your organisational culture, 'I'm here for you, you are important and I have your back. You're not alone and burnout is not a sign of weakness'. Hearing words to this effect coming from your direct manager can have a huge impact on someone who is suffering from burnout.
- **Explicitly encourage everyone to speak up when they are feeling overwhelmed or exhausted.** Once again, respond with compassion and empathy when they do.
- **Avoid labelling and be aware of the language you use.** 'Nut job',

'lightweight', 'unstable', 'soft'. Language matters. So be aware of what words and phrases you use when referring to people's experience of stress and other mental distress.

- **Become aware of your own unconscious bias around mental illness.** Although burnout is not officially classed as a mental illness, as we mentioned earlier, the WHO has titled it an occupational phenomenon. What attitudes do you project about burnout, stress or mental illness? How do you come across to employees on these topics? One study showed that perceived stigma about burnout may reflect the inaccurate belief that most people view burned-out individuals as less competent than those who are not burned out.

WHAT INDIVIDUALS CAN DO TO DESTIGMATISE BURNOUT

Although more responsibility for destigmatising burnout lies with organisations and leaders, all employees can play a role in reducing the stigma around mental distress and burnout. Here are some ideas:

- **If you notice a colleague is struggling or stressed, reach out and ask them how they are—and then be present to listen.** The New Zealand Mental Health Foundation website (www.mentalhealth.org.nz) is a great place to start if you're worried about a colleague and are not sure how to assist. Mentemia is another great resource. It is an app that coaches wellbeing.
- **If it feels safe to do so, speak up about the importance of mental wellness in the workplace.** Ask your direct manager, and whoever is responsible for HR in your organisation, what systems,

processes and policies they have to ensure mental wellbeing and to tackle stress. Know that many of your work colleagues will be experiencing mental distress in the workplace—and will silently thank you for you doing this.

- **Use the abundance of research (including this book) to make your case.** Often leaders will respond to external research or the impact on the bottom line of burnout. But don't just come with problems. Offer up solutions for how your organisation might destigmatise burnout and other mental distress.
- **When considering the key decision-makers in your organisation, take into account how and by what they're influenced.** For some leaders, it might be people and culture, for others, it might be hard facts and figures. Use the WIIFM ('what's in it for me?') approach when stating your ideas and making the case for destigmatising burnout in your organisation.

- **When there are employee engagement surveys or you're asked for feedback on culture or ways your organisation can improve, use this chance to bring mental wellbeing to the fore.** Many organisational surveys provide ways for this to be done anonymously, if you don't feel comfortable doing so directly.
- **Share articles with your direct manager and team mates on mental health and burnout, especially if they pertain to your industry.** Make a case for good mental health improving performance and the bottom line. Suggest ways that your team may be able to incorporate these ideas into the team's operating rhythms. Remember, you don't have to wait until you have the title of leader or manager to demonstrate leadership. You can take proactive approaches to destigmatising burnout in your team. Be the leader you aspire to be.

In conclusion, one of the best resources I've come across in New

Zealand when it comes to destigmatising and addressing workplace mental wellbeing is the website run by the Mental Health Foundation, www.mentalhealth.org.nz. It's full of practical ideas, resources and tips for organisations, leaders and individuals, so check it out. And as I mentioned earlier, the Mentemia app is another great resource for organisations and individuals alike.

KEY TAKEOUTS

- Like most mental distress in the workplace, burnout is shrouded in shame and stigma. This not only stops people from admitting they're suffering from burnout, it also prevents them from asking for help—and this in turn makes it difficult to measure, address and stop it. One of the most important things we can do to stamp out burnout is to reduce the stigma surrounding it. This goes for all mental distress in the workplace, which is more common than you might think.
- Leaders and those at the top of an organisation have an important part to play in destigmatising burnout.

Speaking openly and often about mental wellbeing and their own journeys when it comes to stress and mental wellness is one way. So too is focusing purposefully on creating psychologically safe and trusting environments where it isn't career-limiting for people to share their mental wellbeing challenges. Finally, including mental wellbeing in policies, communication and organisational measurements is also critical to destigmatising burnout.

- We can all play our part in destigmatising mental distress and burnout in our workplaces, even at an individual level. Reaching out and connecting with co-workers and asking if they are OK, practising active listening and encouraging our workplaces to put mental wellbeing on the strategic agenda are all ways we can do this.

CHAPTER 9

SOCIALISE

'I define connection as the energy that exists between people when they feel seen, heard, and valued; when they can give and receive without judgment; and when they derive sustenance and strength from the relationship.'

Brené Brown

Loneliness has a bigger impact on our longevity than obesity, drinking or even smoking. Social connection is up there with oxygen when it comes to how important it is to our survival.

We humans are hardwired to connect with each other. Belonging to some 'tribe'—whether that be family or another group we identify with and feel we belong to—has been crucial for our existence since we were cave-dwellers. We needed to connect to survive and thrive back then; we need to connect to survive and thrive just as much now.

The research on this is telling.

Sarah Pressman from the University of California conducted research on the impact of loneliness—and the results might surprise you. Her study showed that while obesity reduces longevity by 20 per cent, drinking alcohol by 30 per cent and smoking by 50 per cent, loneliness has the biggest impact of all: it reduces longevity by a staggering 70 per cent! The good news is that the opposite is also true. This same study demonstrated that feelings of social connection can *lower* rates of anxiety and depression, *boost* our immune system and *lengthen* our life.

Add to that the fact that a meta study of over 148 studies (with more than 308,000 participants) indicated that individuals with stronger social relationships had a 50 per cent increased likelihood of survival in modern times.

It's unquestionable that we need social connections in order to thrive. And given most of us spend the majority of our waking hours at work, it follows that social connection at work is incredibly important.

Unfortunately, loneliness is on the rise, particularly in Western societies. The 2018 Australian Loneliness Report found that one in four Australians reported feeling lonely each week, while leaders at the World Economic Forum in Switzerland in January 2020 were told that 40 per cent of those under 25 globally are lonely.

Similarly, the General Social Survey in the US found that the number of Americans with no close friends has tripled since 1985. 'Zero' is the most common number of confidants, reported by almost a quarter of those surveyed. That's scary: *a quarter of people said they did not have anyone in whom they could confide.* Likewise, the average number of people Americans feel they can talk to about 'important matters' has fallen from three to two.

The 2016 New Zealand General Social Survey found that 650,000 New Zealanders felt lonely at least some of the time, and, of those, 15–24-year-olds were the most affected. In just two years, between 2014 and 2016, the estimated number of Kiwis (aged 15+) who felt lonely all or most of the time increased by 70 per cent, from 140,000 to 240,000.

Why is this? It seems that although we're more connected through things like social media, we're doing less of the real connection stuff. Face-to-face connection, and real relationships that bring deep connection, seem to be less common than they used to be. Communication may be easier and faster these days —only a mere text or email away. But that doesn't necessarily imply true connection.

It's not just at a societal level that we're feeling more isolated, either. It's happening in our workplaces, too.

A recent study by Australian HR think tank Reventure of just over 1000 employees found that 37 per cent feel lonely at work. And a 2014 survey by Relate, the UK's leading relationship support organisation, revealed that 42 per cent of British workers studied don't have a single friend at the office.

If you think all this talk of social connection being important in the workplace is a bit soft and overrated, there are proven links between social connection and performance. As revealed in a *Fast Company* article, one study showed that individuals who were given 15 minutes to socialise with colleagues had a 20 per cent increase in performance over their peers who didn't. Another study found that 38 per cent of lonely workers reported making more mistakes, and 40 per cent felt less productive. Lonely workers perform worse in their roles, causing impaired creativity, productivity and decision-making.

It follows, then, that loneliness and a sense of social isolation are not just hurting individuals at work; they are also hurting our organisations. According to the EY Belonging Barometer, 40 per cent of employees in the US feel isolated in their role, which is driving higher disengagement and lower productivity. According to a *Harvard Business Review* article, 'Burnout at Work Isn't Just About Exhaustion. It's Also About Loneliness', companies with high disengagement and loneliness experience almost 37 per cent higher absenteeism, 49 per cent more accidents and 16 per cent lower profitability than those with high engagement.

WHAT'S DRIVING THIS INCREASE IN LONELINESS AND ISOLATION IN OUR WORKPLACES?

There are a number of factors, some of which are double-edged swords. Some new developments have brought improved working conditions, but they've also contributed to a greater sense of isolation at work. For example, the rise in different and new communication technologies, while improving communication and efficiencies in many cases, also means that face-to-face contact at work is diminishing. The Covid-19 pandemic has impacted on this even further.

Flexible working arrangements have brought an immense number of benefits to both organisations and employees, but they have meant that there are fewer people working together. Globalisation and the increase in remote-working teams have also had an impact. There's been growth in jobs where people are working autonomously and mostly on their own, such as those in the IT sector, over recent years.

Finally, heavier workloads often contribute to less time for non-task-related communication or social connection activities at work. Part-time workers (parents spring to mind) may be more prone to this, as they focus on getting their tasks done when they are at work and have less time for 'water cooler' conversations. Because of the 'hard stop' many have at the end of their day, where they must leave at a certain time, or because of their reduced hours overall, they often feel that there is less time for 'non-essential' socialising at work.

THE LINK BETWEEN ISOLATION AT WORK AND BURNOUT

Isolation and loneliness (either perceived or real) is one of the major causes of burnout, as we outlined in Chapter 5.

This link doesn't go just one way. There's a nasty little twist to the link between isolation and burnout. As well as isolation *causing* burnout, isolation can also be *caused by* the exhaustion felt by someone experiencing burnout. So isolation can cause burnout—and burnout can cause isolation.

When we're beginning to feel burned out, we stop attending social events with colleagues. We withdraw from conversations. The relationship is both reciprocal and intertwined. When I was in the throes of burnout, I found myself disengaging from social connection at work that I'd previously sought. It exacerbated my sense of loneliness and isolation as a leader. And, as Emma Seppälä and Marissa King pointed out in their *Harvard Business Review* article 'Burnout at Work Isn't Just About Exhaustion. It's Also About Loneliness', 'There is a significant correlation between feeling lonely and work exhaustion: the more people are exhausted, the lonelier they feel.'

On top of this, there's a risk that if we're burned out, we think it's all tickety-boo for everyone else. We're likely to feel more isolated if we believe everyone else is coping with their work—and we're not. And because of the stigma attached to burnout, this too can be a vicious circle.

As we now know, isolation is a major cause of burnout. Being able to talk to someone about the tough things we are experiencing at work (like stress) goes a long way to protecting us from feeling isolated. And yet, just 34 per cent of respondents in the Cogo Workplace Wellbeing Survey 2020 said they could talk to someone in a management/leadership/HR role about the stress they experienced at work. Thirty-nine per cent said they can talk to someone else at work but not someone in a management/leadership/HR role. And 21 per cent (nearly a quarter) said they had *no one* at work that they talk to about the stress they experience.

It gets worse. In the Cogo survey, 45 per cent of those reporting having no one to talk to were not coping well with that stress, while just 18 per cent of those who were able to talk to a manager/leader/HR person said they weren't coping well. ('Not coping well' sat at 33 per cent for those who could talk to someone else—i.e. not a manager, but a colleague).

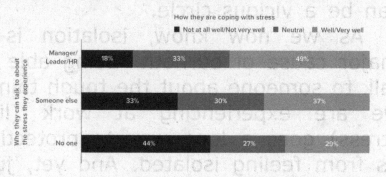

Figure 3: The impact of being able to talk to someone about stress on how well respondents feel they can cope with the stress that they experience at work (Cogo Workplace Wellbeing Survey 2020)

We need to change these statistics. We want our people to be able to talk to someone in a leadership role or to someone who is in a position to do something about the stressed employee's experiences. These numbers also indicate that there's a lot going on around stress in our workplaces that leaders aren't aware of. And that's not good either.

WHAT CAN WE DO TO PREVENT ISOLATION AT WORK?

Having genuine personal connections at work can buffer us significantly against burnout. While many organisations and leaders leave this largely up to their employees to create, that's a mistake.

Fostering social connections, creating trusting environments and encouraging more meaningful and safe communication should be one of an organisation's key priorities.

This is where leaders can make a significant impact on reducing burnout—by creating cultures within their teams that foster relatedness and social connection. In particular, this is about creating an environment of trust and inclusion within your team. Even a leader's individual relational energy—that is, the extent to which their interactions with others either motivate and invigorate, or drain and exhaust—can have a significant effect on the isolation element of burnout.

So what are some specific things that we can do to *socialise,* the third strategy to combat burnout? Let's start at the macro level, the organisation, as that's where the most significant influence lever comes into play.

WHAT ORGANISATIONS CAN DO TO BUILD SOCIAL CONNECTION AT WORK

- **Purposefully encourage social connection.** The first thing organisations can do is to create conditions in the workplace that purposefully encourage social connection. This means proactively investing in social connection. And I don't mean just starting up a company football team, although that might be one example. This is about looking at how your systems, policies and culture ('the way things are done around here') either foster and encourage meaningful connection between your employees or, conversely, allow isolation to take hold.

This can be a challenge for many executive leadership teams, because it often means investing in programmes or approaches that may not have an immediate or short-term ROI (return on investment), but will have significant positive effects in the long term by preventing employees becoming isolated and burned out.

—Take peer coaching, for example. Formal peer coaching programmes are where employees at a peer level, from different parts of the organisation, come together on a regular basis to share challenges and solutions, as well as get coached by their peers in a structured way. Peer coaching groups not only improve a variety of professional skills for the participants, but they also connect peers in a meaningful way, combatting isolation and reducing stress. I have led leadership programmes that use peer coaching, and overwhelmingly, participants report this to be hugely effective for building cross-functional connection, breaking down silos and addressing the sometimes isolating feelings associated with leadership.

—It's especially important for executive leadership teams to be intentional in building social connection during and immediately after a period of change, whether that be restructuring, downsizing or even massive growth. That's because increased levels of change are more likely to negatively affect worker wellbeing. For example, one meta study looking at the impact of restructuring on employee wellbeing found that restructuring events, either with or without staff reductions, mainly have a negative impact on the wellbeing of employees.

The way an organisation can go about mitigating this phenomenon may be as simple as providing safe platforms for employees to share their experiences and feelings during the change. Or it might include focusing leaders on providing increased support and two-way communication during these times.

There's often a focus on those who may be losing their jobs (if that's the case), but it's just as important to ensure good social connection and support is there for those remaining. Remember, every time someone leaves or joins a team, it becomes in effect a 'new' team. The team dynamics change. And, therefore, this is a time to be more deliberate about building trust and social connection.

- **Look at the use of technology in your organisation with a social-connection lens.** The use of technology can enable social connection, but if not used purposefully, or if it's overused, it can hinder it. Like most organisational tools, it's how you apply it that counts.

—And it seems technology can have an impact just by its mere presence. Research by Andrew K. Przybylski and Netta Weinstein of the University of Essex demonstrated that simply having a phone nearby caused pairs of strangers to rate their conversation as less meaningful, their conversation partners as less empathetic and their new relationship as less close than strangers with a notebook nearby instead.

This research gives us another powerful reason to put down our phone, step away from our computers and give someone our full attention when they're speaking to us. This is especially important for leaders. We all know the powerful impact of receiving someone's full, undivided attention. It's as rare as it is connecting. This becomes even more powerful when it's your direct manager who's doing this.

—A company's use of technology and its protocols is relevant not only for remote teams. For example, an organisation that has a culture of 'always on', where leaders send emails (and expect responses) late at night or within unrealistic timeframes as the cultural norm, can also contribute to stress and overwork for employees. This practice sends a strong message about working culture. One simple way to address this is to set limits on technology, such as restricting the use of mobile phones during meetings or reducing emails and other work communication outside of work hours.

—On the other hand, technology can play a major role in connecting employees and building social connection. It's clear that Covid-19 is redefining society's relationship with everyday technologies that make socialisation possible. Zoom, Slack, Microsoft Teams and a host of other technology platforms can be very powerful connectors of employees. Once again, it's how you use them. If it's a big group, then the ability to break out into smaller groups for discussion will improve connection and involvement of those who are on the call.

—Working across time zones can exacerbate social isolation. This is where technology can also be our friend. As Melissa Lamson, an expert on leading virtual teams, suggests, 'Make a point of intentionally connecting with the people in your team three times as often as you do with the people you see spontaneously in the office. This effort will pay off for you in increased engagement and strong connections with each of your team members.'

- **Be more purposeful about how communication takes place in your organisation.** Make in-person the default communication when there is any potential for conflict or where social connection is paramount to the success of the encounter. If it's not possible to communicate in person, then via video is the next best option. If that's not possible, opt for phone. Of course, email and text may both necessarily be the right form of communication in many instances, but as communication media, these are more often than not overused. There are too many examples of when email is used, when face-to-face communication would improve not only social connection, but also productivity and effectiveness. Too often, we hide behind email or written communication, which creates a veritable melting-pot of misunderstanding. Doing so increases the chance that interpersonal conflict will grow, instead of being resolved.

- **Start social connection at the top table.** If a leadership team is dysfunctional and lacking in approaches that build and foster social connection and trust, then it's going to be harder to build social connection throughout the rest of the organisation. As a leadership coach, I tend to work mostly with senior leadership teams, and I have seen profoundly positive effects which have flowed on to the entire organisation when the leadership team works on this stuff. When a leadership team starts to see the benefits of purposefully building social connection, establishing trust and taking an inclusive approach with *this* team, they start to see the power of encouraging this approach throughout the entire organisation.

—It can be tough. There's lots to do and get on with. Problems to fix, strategy to execute, external forces to navigate, important tasks to complete. There are way more 'what are we doing?' than 'how are we going?' conversations at this level. And for the most part, that's cool. Stuff needs to get done. But those leadership teams who make time for 'how are we going?' as well as 'what are we doing?' conversations not only perform better, they stamp out stress and isolation within the leadership team.

—We must first model what we want to see in others. Being purposeful at building social connection at a leadership level is a powerful way for leadership teams to model social connection. Never be fooled—your people can tell when the senior team has connection and when it doesn't. While having this connection won't guarantee success in the rest of the organisation, its absence won't derail you before you even start.

- **Get serious about stamping out destructive workplace politics and bullying.**
'*I work for a government agency where middle management on-site is toxic and has a culture of bullying. The work stress I can handle—it is part of the job. The toxic nature of the office—unhealthy and stressful. I am one of seven people looking for other work due to this.*'

Respondent, Cogo Workplace Wellbeing Survey 2020

—Workplace politics and bullying are like lighterfuel for isolation in our workplaces. In the Cogo Workplace Wellbeing Survey 2020, workplace politics and the behaviour of colleagues or managers featured among the top five stressors for both men and women.

—The presence of bullying is associated with an increase in burnout, so you must take a very proactive approach at an organisational level to create psychological trust. Stamping out any bullying or workplace discrimination is an important step for all organisations to take.

—This kind of behaviour can be hard to spot, and concentrating on your core daily business tasks can take up all of your energy. But here are three obvious but effective ways to start:

1. Be loud and vocal about having a zero-tolerance policy for bullying and harassment. Make sure the consequences of this behaviour are clear and followed through.

2. Have a clearly communicated, neutral grievance policy that employees can pursue if they have concerns. It's not surprising that many people feel uncomfortable about reporting issues like this to their direct manager. Communicate this at key points—especially when people first join the company (especially important for leaders) and train leaders on anti-bullying behaviour and discrimination.

3. Ensure your leaders understand that the most important

priority they have—before turning their attention to the work at hand—is to create trust with and within the team they lead. Everything else positive flows from this core building block. Train them on how to do this.

- **Utilise the power of coaching and mentoring.** Another strategy is to provide mentoring and coaching support, particularly at critical junctures, such as when you are onboarding or inducting first-time leaders. Coaching has proven to have some pretty impressive results, whether that's through peer coaching, internal or external coaches. A global ICF study showed 80 per cent of people who receive coaching report increased self-confidence, and over 70 per cent benefit from improved work performance and relationships, and more effective communication skills. Eighty-six per cent of companies report that they recouped their investment in coaching and more.

WHAT LEADERS CAN DO TO BUILD SOCIAL CONNECTION AT WORK

Once again, the impact of the relationship between a direct report and their manager plays a huge role when it comes to burnout. Showing you care for your direct reports is critical. Take these statistics from the Cogo Workplace Wellbeing Survey 2020:

Those who feel that their direct manager genuinely cares about their mental wellbeing are:
- less likely to show signs of exhaustion (49 per cent versus 61 per cent for the whole sample)
- less likely to show signs of isolation (15 per cent versus 30 per cent)
- less likely to show signs of a lack of engagement (38 per cent versus 57 per cent)
- less likely to take leave because of stress (23 per cent versus 34 per cent).

It's not just at the organisational level where we can improve social connection and, by doing so, buffer against burnout. Individual leaders at *all* levels within an organisation can have a massive impact on this burnout-buffering strategy. So if you're a leader of people, what can you do when it comes to the *socialise* strategy?

- **Start with building trust.** If you're a leader of people, focus first and foremost on building trust within the team you lead. The importance of trust cannot be overlooked for team leadership, whether you are working to build conditions for social connection or high performance. As well as being a building block for high performance, trust within a team creates a wall of protection from isolation.

  —Building this trust is about the willingness of each team member to be vulnerable with each other (and with you) when it comes to their work and their membership in the team. In other words, do all team members feel safe to share their worries, their mistakes, their weaknesses and their challenges with the other members of the team and with you? Are they comfortable to speak up and offer their opinions?

—When we talk about building social connection in this context it's called 'affective trust'. This is a form of trust based on emotional bonds and interpersonal relatedness. It varies from 'cognitive trust', which springs from reliability and competence.

—Creating trust starts with the leader—you. This means you must go first. You've got to model a certain level of vulnerability and opening up. As Ken Blanchard, global management expert and author of *The One Minute Manager,* says, 'When you open up and share about yourself, you demonstrate a vulnerability that engenders trust.' There are many specific tools for how leaders can create trust in their teams, which are covered in Appendix J.

- **Have 'how are we going?' conversations.** Ensure you're having 'how are we going?' conversations, as well as 'what are we doing?' conversations. Focus not only on the task at hand, but also on the relationship between the person and their direct manager and the wellbeing of the person charged with the task. This can be as simple as asking your team as a whole 'What do we need to keep doing, stop doing or start doing to improve our working relationships or team performance?' And it can be as unassuming as enquiring (and being genuinely interested in) your direct reports' wellbeing on a regular basis. Ask a version of 'How are you doing?' and follow this with your full presence and active listening. Listening to understand, not to reply, even for a few minutes, can invite a deeper conversation. Appendix D has an outline of a one-on-one meeting structure that will help you to incorporate this approach.

—Make sure you're not falling into the trap where work is taking place at such a break-neck pace that members of your team barely have time to get a cup of coffee, let alone have a meaningful conversation with their co-worker.

- **Put your own connection oxygen mask on.** Ensure that you build your *own* professional social connections at work and in your role as a leader. As that overused but useful metaphor suggests, it's important that you put on your own oxygen mask before you help others. Burnout can be contagious (the term used in the research is 'crossover'), and leaders who are burned out can 'infect' a team in much the same way as if they showed up to work with the flu. So it's important that you take steps (like reading this book!) to safeguard yourself from burnout and build social connections that work for you in your professional life.
- **Give and seek regular feedback.** Offer FAST (frequent, accurate, specific, timely) feedback. In fact, research suggests we should give three times more positive and valuing feedback than corrective feedback. People need to know that they're valued and that their

contributions are generally positive. So, shine a light on what you want to see grow in those you lead. The worst thing you can do is give people no feedback at all. That's isolation-building. Look at systems, symbols and your own feedback-giving and-receiving skills when it comes to two-way, informal feedback within your team, not just formal feedback. And make constructive feedback a learning-focused, two-way conversation.

- **Pay attention to induction and team-building sessions.** Take a careful look at how you bring people onto your team. This not only means getting them up to speed on the task-related aspects of their job, but also how you integrate your new team member into your team in terms of social and relational aspects. What you decide to do will vary depending on your organisational culture, but you might assign them a mentor or buddy within the team, or organise regular, informal catch-ups or coffees with yourself and other members of the team—not with any formal agenda, but just to listen and see how they're going in those early, crucial months. Or it might be redoing some of the team-building activities that you have done with your current team to include new members, too.

- **Spend time connecting together on team dynamics and higher-level strategic issues.** I personally don't like the term 'team-building days', as it conjures up doing naff activities that make people cringe. That's not what I'm talking about here. Rather, spending at least one or two days a year away from the office, to focus on assessing and improving how your team is working together, with specific actions following these sessions. This not only builds social connection, it improves team performance as well, provided it's designed and facilitated well. I run leadership workshops like this for executive leadership teams, and most will lament on the first day or leading up to the sessions that they don't have time to do it. But I have yet to have anyone say afterwards that it was not a worthwhile investment of their time.

- **Take a look at some of the organisational ideas above and see how you could implement some of these (such as peer coaching) at a team level.** Gallup research found that the single best predictor of higher wellbeing and engagement was 'not what people are doing—but *who* they are with'. So small steps to make space for social connection within your team can pay big dividends.
- **Always and continually focus on improving your self-awareness and emotional intelligence.** Scientists have found that emotions are contagious in the workplace: employees feel emotionally depleted just by watching unpleasant interactions between co-workers. This starts with you as a leader. Work on building your emotional intelligence. Daniel Goleman is the world expert in this area and some

resources on how to build your emotional intelligence are listed in Appendix H.
- **Do little things that build connection with your direct reports.** This can be as simple as smiling and connecting with people, regularly practising active listening, calling people by their name and taking an interest in their interests, or remembering the names of their family members.

WHAT INDIVIDUALS CAN DO TO BUILD SOCIAL CONNECTION AT WORK

> *'If you think you are too small to be effective, you have never been in the dark with a mosquito.'*
> Betty Reese

Although the conditions for social connection are largely dictated by leaders and the organisation, organisations are made up of people! There are definite steps that individuals can take to build and engender social connection in their organisation. Let's dive into what you, as an individual within an organisation or team, can do to practise the strategy of *socialise*.

- **Find out what is available at your organisation and within your team, then connect socially in a way that works for you.** It can be easy to see social activities at work as being in the 'I don't have time/too hard' basket, especially if you're stretched as it is or you work part-time. It's also worth noting that some of us need more social connection than others—what works for a social-butterfly extrovert who sees relationships at work as paramount will be very different to the social connection needs of an introverted, task-oriented and less socially disposed colleague. You do you! But if you find yourself feeling disconnected, isolated or alone in any capacity at work, this might indicate an opportunity for you to develop deeper, more meaningful connections at work. When I say 'deeper, more meaningful connections', I'm not implying you have to have deep and personal conversations with everyone. Research has indicated that just one meaningful friendship or connection with a co-worker in whom you can confide is enough.

- **Go first.** This is an idea espoused by Gabby Reece, an American professional volleyball player, sports announcer and fashion model, whose thoughts I read in Tim Ferris's book *Tools of Titans*. Her approach offers an idea for building social connections at work. Reece talks about 'always going first'. She says, 'I always say that I'll go first. If I'm coming across somebody and make eye contact, I'll smile first.' Whether it's striking up a conversation in the staff kitchen and asking someone about their role, bringing in some baking (food always seems to be a great connector!) or asking someone who seems to be on their own to join you and your usual crew to get some lunch, don't be afraid to make the first move. Here's a cool thing, too: social connection can have benefits for the person who goes first, as well as the recipient of their kindness. A study by the University of Columbia showed that people who engaged in pro-social behaviour with social 'weak ties' in their lives—i.e. co-workers they didn't know that well, or people in their lunchtime fitness class—reported less loneliness and a higher level of happiness than people who avoided unnecessary conversation.

- **Connect with others in your organisation via social groups.** For some people, work-sponsored sports teams are the way to go. For others, being a member of a social committee might be more your cup of tea. If your organisation doesn't have anything like this, there's no reason you couldn't start something up—it doesn't have to be a big deal. One smaller company I work with has a weekly quiz that lasts about ten minutes. There's always lots of laughter when they do it. Another firm has awards given out to employees each month under a theme, recognising little achievements or challenges their people have overcome in a humorous way.

- **Don't underestimate your ability to influence your direct manager.** You could make some suggestions regarding how to improve your meetings, or ideas for what to cover in your one-on-one catch-up with your direct manager. One client of mine came up with the suggestion of starting their meeting with a quick-fire wellbeing check-in that lasted five minutes. Her manager loved this idea and the whole team has reported a greater sense of trust and connection as a result.

—You don't need to wait for your manager to come up with initiatives. As a team, you could brainstorm ideas for greater social connection. As a leader, I loved it when my team would take responsibility for ideas on how to improve our team trust and connection rather than stand back and wait for me to fill the void—or, worse, complain but not come up with potential ideas and solutions.

KEY TAKEOUTS

- Research shows us that, around the globe, we are lonelier than ever before—and this is happening in our workplaces, too.
- Isolation (either perceived or real) is a key cause of burnout. Being purposeful about creating social connection within our workplaces is key to fighting isolation.
- Building trust—within teams, between employees and the organisation, and between leaders and their teams—is a priority when it comes to the socialisation strategy. There are things that organisations as a whole, leaders and individuals can all do to increase social connection in the workplace, which are outlined in this chapter.

CHAPTER 10

ORGANISE

'It is not enough to be busy. So are the ants.'
                              Henry David Thoreau

In Western society, we are worshipping at the altar of busyness. This noxious 'cult of the busy' is omnipresent at a societal level and it has seeped into many of our organisational cultures, too. Even at an individual level, it has spread into our psyches. The idea that work is inherently virtuous and that, conversely, rest is inherently lazy or bad is a commonly held one.

How often have you asked someone how they are and have heard the reply 'Crazy busy!'? So often, we wear our busyness and overwork as badges of honour. In some cases, we even get caught up in glorifying stress. It's worse in certain professions where busyness and overwork are seen as the hallmarks of success. I've seen this play out in the legal and other professional services industries, for example. It's expected that working ridiculous hours and getting through huge workloads is the necessary norm to get ahead. I remember one partner of a law firm exclaiming to his team that they had to be in 'beast mode' or be 'an octane-fuelled, always-available player' in order to be part of his team. He worked over 80 hours a week, and he expected his team to do the same.

But research by the Boston Consulting Group of several of their US offices indicated that it's perfectly possible for consultants and other professionals to meet the highest standards of service and still have planned, uninterrupted time off. They even found that when the assumption that everyone needs to be always available was collectively challenged, not only could individuals take time off, but their work actually benefited. These experiments with time off resulted in more open dialogue among team members—a benefit in itself. But the improved communication also sparked new processes that enhanced the teams' ability to work efficiently and effectively.

This societal culture of overwork doesn't appear to be waning, either, even when faced with indisputable statistics that clearly demonstrate the risks to organisations and people of this approach. In fact, in many societies, overwork is on the rise. Take, for example, the Japanese phenomenon of *karoshi*—'occupational sudden death'—that I mentioned earlier in the book. A 2008 Harvard Business School survey of 1000 professionals found that 94 per cent worked 50 hours or more a week, and almost half worked in excess of 65 hours a week.

Our bias for action is alive and well in our mental models about work. Take this interesting and thought-provoking study of professional soccer goalies as an example.

Researchers looked at professional soccer goalkeepers when they defended against penalty kicks. They wanted to find out the most effective strategy for stopping the ball.

You'd think that the goalies would be better off jumping to the right or to the left. You'd be wrong. As it turns out, staying in the centre is the way to go.

The research showed that goalkeepers who dive to the right stop the ball 12.6 per cent of the time, and those who dive to the left do only a little better: they stop the ball 14.2 per cent of the time.

But goalies who don't move? They do the best of all and have a 33.3 per cent chance of stopping the ball!

But here's the kicker (excuse the pun). Despite this fact, goalies stay in the centre only 6.3 per cent of the time! Why? Because it looks and feels better to have missed the ball by diving (an action) in the wrong direction than to watch the ball go sailing by and never have moved (inaction).

It's not just soccer goalies that are afflicted by this action bias, either. Most organisational cultures value *doing* over *being;* pushing forward at all costs over pausing, even when that is what is needed for a moment. They strive for constant growth over periods of consolidation. Reflection and deeper thinking are sometimes not valued as much in organisations as keeping on doing, but they can lead to better outcomes. Board and shareholder expectations do not allow for anything other than bigger and faster and more—each and every year—even when external conditions make it extremely hard to deliver this, or when doing so will be to the detriment of their people's wellbeing. And it's interesting to note that when employees believe their companies think the bottom line is more important than people, there is a 185 per cent increased chance of burnout.

The irony is that we know through countless studies that long hours and overwork diminish both productivity and the quality of our work. As James Surowiecki noted in his *New Yorker* article 'The Cult of Overwork', 'Among industrial workers, overtime raises the rate of mistakes and safety mishaps; likewise, for knowledge workers fatigue and sleep-deprivation make it hard to perform at a high cognitive level.'

He goes on to ask the question, if the benefits of working fewer hours are this clear, why has it been so hard for businesses to embrace the idea? In some cases, it's about economics. Take those professions like law, who generally bill by the hour. Some of the systems can encourage and reward people for working longer, not smarter. When it comes to most knowledge workers, Surowiecki rightly suggests that it can be more difficult to quantify productivity than for those in the manufacturing sector like an assembly-line worker. He references Bob Pozen, the author of *Extreme Productivity,* a book on slashing work hours, '[who] told me, "Time becomes an easy metric to measure how productive someone is, even though it doesn't have any necessary connection to what they achieve."'

THE 'TRYING TO DO TOO MUCH WITHOUT THE RESOURCES TO DO IT' AFFLICTION

There's a related problem to this overwork and busyness culture: it is a pernicious affliction running rampant throughout our organisations, and it's called the 'trying to do too much all at once without the resources to do it' affliction. It's a common one, and unfortunately it affirms the 'cult of busy' idea that is not only valued at a societal level, but also sees many of us deriving some of our self-worth from being busy and needed. Add to this, the reinforcing nature of many organisations' expectations and we find overwhelmed people and teams across almost every industry and profession I've worked with.

I'll give you just one example among the many I have come across in my role as an executive coach. A large corporate I worked with acquired and integrated a major competitor, implemented a new organisation-wide IT system, initiated a substantial cost-saving strategy and undertook a *different* restructure not associated with that first acquisition—all the while navigating some major and unforeseen disruptions to their industry, and all in the space of 12 months. Not surprisingly, many of their managers who I spoke to felt both bewildered and burned out.

Unfortunately, this 'trying to do too much all at once without the adequate resources required to succeed' affliction is common in our workplaces. And it's contributing to one of the biggest causes of burnout—overwork. As the saying goes, 'We tend to overestimate what we can achieve in one year and underestimate what we can achieve in five.'

Jason Fried, co-founder and president of Basecamp, a management and team-communication tool used by thousands of companies worldwide, wrote in his great book *It Doesn't Have to Be Crazy at Work*:

> *'If the only way you can inspire the troops is by a regimen of exhaustion, it's time to look for some deeper substance. Because what trickles down is less likely to be admiration but dread and fear instead. A leader who sets an example of self-sacrifice can't help but ask self-sacrifice of others.'*

Therefore, in this chapter we dive into the final antidote to burnout—*organise*.

> *'I'm not sure how effective it is to be offered yoga, exercises, and mindfulness at work when the structure of your workplace is rigid, inflexible and micromanaged and the workload is heavy.'*
> Respondent, Cogo Workplace Wellbeing Survey 2020

Of all the 'burnout busters', the strategy of *organise,* which encapsulates one of the most pivotal organisational skills, prioritisation, perhaps packs the biggest punch of all when it comes to preventing burnout. Why? Because how we organise and prioritise what gets done in our organisation creates a massive lever on employee activity—what they do, the quality of their work, how many hours they work and even the relationship they have towards their work, their colleagues and the organisation itself. And this isn't just about individuals honing their organisational skills, either—it is a strategy that must be looked at with an organisational lens.

Many executive teams, like the one I spoke of trying to do all those things at once, underestimate the flow-on effect of a significant new project, strategic shift or major organisational initiative on people's existing workloads throughout the organisation. This is exacerbated when those projects and initiatives are viewed in a vacuum. When leaders do not see the systemic and intertwined relationships between organisational initiatives, they overlook the flow-on effects, particularly as those impacts trickle further down the chain.

Middle management is often hardest hit. Research has shown that middle managers are often more prone to overwork than employees at either end of the organisational hierarchy. As authors Eric M. Anicich and Jacob B. Hirsh point out in their *Harvard Business Review* article 'Why Being a Middle Manager is So Exhausting', 'By virtue of their structural positions, they are simultaneously the "victims and the carriers of change" within an organization, receiving strategy prescriptions from their bosses above and having to implement those strategies with the people who work beneath them. As a result, middle managers often find themselves stuck in-between various stakeholder groups.' The result is that those middle managers are often in the middle—facing conflicting demands and ongoing pressures.

It's stating the obvious, but trying to do too much with too few resources—or with unrealistic deadlines—can contribute to burnout. Excessive workloads and working too hard for too long on a regular basis are major culprits in the burnout battle.

The prevalence of constant restructuring and downsizing (that's likely to increase following Covid-19) can also lead to work overload. This is because often people are expected to do more with less, more often.

Recent McKinsey Global research, surveying a large set of executives worldwide, suggests that many companies these days are in a nearly permanent state of organisational flux. Almost 60 per cent of the respondents, for example, said they had experienced a redesign within the past two years, and an additional 25 per cent said they experienced a redesign three or more years ago. A generation or two back, most executives might have experienced some sort of organisational upheaval just a few times over the course of their careers.

The flow-on effects of this high rate of downsizing and restructures can leave employees doing more with less. In a Harvard research study, researchers found that: downsizing firms lose valuable knowledge when employees exit; remaining employees struggle to manage increased workloads, leaving little time to learn new skills; and remaining employees lose trust in management, resulting in less engagement and loyalty.

I'm not dissing restructuring per se. A need to be nimble and to adjust organisational structures to meet the environment are necessary and warranted. But we need to pay close attention to the impacts they have on people and be more purposeful in providing support when we make these changes.

So, I'm stating the obvious when I say that one of the best antidotes to burnout is for leaders to get better at organising work. This includes self-evident activities such as prioritisation, but also extends to the amount of control workers have over *how* they do their role. As we covered earlier in the book when we spoke about Self Determination Theory (see section entitled "WHAT CAUSES BURNOUT?"), a sense of autonomy is huge for motivation. It also means ensuring people have sufficient resources to do the tasks they've been charged with.

It's time we give up the belief that we need to be constantly working in order to be successful. Perpetual work without rest—metaphorically or literally, individually as well as organisationally—at first glance might seem like a stupid thing to do and something that shouldn't take place. But common sense is clearly not so common when considering the prevailing statistics on overwork and high stress around the world. The wisest organisations are beginning to embrace the concept that rest, recovery and reflection are critical components to thrive—alongside action, effort and hard work.

'ORGANISE' APPLIED AT THE MACRO AND THE MICRO LEVEL

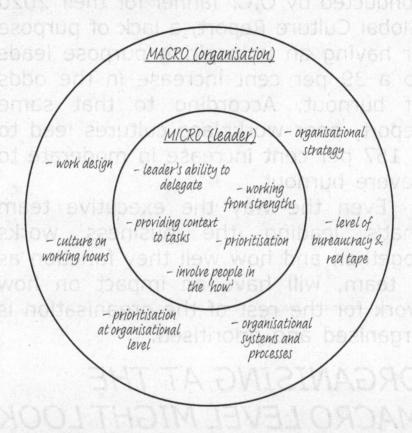

When it comes to applying the *organise* strategy within organisations to combat burnout, we can do this on both a macro, strategic level and a micro or individual level.

The macro level considers how work is organised in an organisation as a whole. It applies to organisational strategy, purpose, systems, processes and even organisational culture. For example, according to research conducted by O.C. Tanner for their 2020 Global Culture Report, a lack of purpose or having an uninspiring purpose leads to a 39 per cent increase in the odds of burnout. According to that same report, poor workplace cultures lead to a 157 per cent increase in moderate to severe burnout.

Even the way the executive team that's leading the business works together, and how well they function as a team, will have an impact on how work for the rest of the organisation is organised and prioritised.

ORGANISING AT THE MACRO LEVEL MIGHT LOOK LIKE:

- Improving your work design—the degree to which people within your organisation have a say in the way that their work is carried out. You

need to look at this from a cultural, as well as process, perspective.
- The executive team's approach to organisational prioritising. An executive team's organisational strategy and key priorities for the next two years will have an exponential impact on prioritisation and workload throughout the business. Limit your strategic pillars or key strategic imperatives to three to five. If work doesn't fit into these, don't do it.
- Looking at organisational processes and systems—whether task-allocation processes clearly identify the resources employees need to do their jobs or whether this is overlooked, left to chance or not clearly measured.
- The level of bureaucracy and red tape in an organisation—the weeds that clutter the path towards achieving organisational goals.

As I've said, it's not only at the macro level that we need to apply the *organise* strategy. It also applies at the micro level. Individual leaders at all levels within an organisation can (and do) have a substantial impact on their team's workflow and workload. A manager's individual behaviour, skills and mindset when it comes to organising work can either increase or decrease the likelihood of their people experiencing burnout.

ORGANISING AT THE MICRO LEVEL MIGHT LOOK LIKE:

- A manager's ability to delegate effectively, to sift and sort through the inevitable white noise of organisational life and clearly define and communicate priorities to their team. This refers as much to what *not* to do as it does to *what* to do.
- Whether a leader provides context to tasks when assigning them, or whether instructions are given without explanation of why they're important or how this person's work is contributing to the team's or organisation's goals or strategy.
- A team leader's focus on the wellbeing of their team—whether

they ensure their direct reports work reasonable hours and whether they regularly assess and discuss their teams' workloads effectively. Also, whether they themselves model 'overwork' or 'balance'.

How a leader leads his or her team when it comes to the *organise* strategy can have a massive impact on whether burnout flounders or flourishes, regardless of the macro forces at play. And an organisation's processes, culture and strategy sway this burnout dial, regardless of individual leader competence.

HOW CAN WE UTILISE THE 'ORGANISE' STRATEGY?

Given the macro and micro forces affecting how work is organised, what are some practical tools and approaches that leaders, organisations (and even individual employees) can adopt to organise work more effectively in a way that reduces burnout and increases both engagement and productivity? Let's take a look...

WHAT ORGANISATIONS CAN DO TO ORGANISE

- **Before you take on a new initiative that is companywide, consider what else is going on in the organisation at the time.** What is happening external to the organisation? What impact will these external market-forces have when it comes to taking on a company initiative? Avoid looking at a new organisation-wide initiative in isolation. Instead, consider the impact on your people's workloads in a systemic way. Don't fall into the trap of trying to do too much all at once. Force yourself to keep organisational priorities to a minimum. Which leads me to this next point...
- Priority comes from the English word 'prior' and means 'one'. **Get exceptionally clear on the single most important priority or theme for your organisation for the coming year.** Patrick Lencioni, author of *The Five Dysfunctions of*

a Team, calls this a 'thematic goal' or rallying cry.

—This concept is simple to grasp but difficult to execute. It's worth the effort, however, and it has brought positive results to executive leadership teams that I have worked with. Assuming that there will be metrics that are always going to be important—profit, revenue and market share, for example—by all means measure and focus on these continuously. But get clear on the *one big key thrust* or initiative relevant to the whole company, then make this the focal point for a period of time.

—Communicate this one rallying cry until you're blue in the face. Resist the 'kinda interesting or important' other ideas or initiatives. Be laser-focused in what you take on as an organisation. Ditch or delay the rest. If you must go ahead with another major organisational initiative, try piloting it first in a small part of the organisation, rather than assuming a fullscale rollout is the only way to go.

- **Assess whether you have a culture of overwork within your organisation, and aim to reduce it if you do.** Take a closer look at your systems, symbols and common behaviours through this 'overwork' lens. Do you link performance to number of hours worked—or output? Does your culture reward working long hours, or do you encourage employees to take regular breaks—whether that be on a daily, weekly or annual basis? Are there systems and symbols within your company that encourage overwork? Take a closer look at your policies and, more importantly, your culture, around what hours people are expected to work in order to get the job done. What are your approaches to the use of technology? Is it commonplace for work emails to be sent outside of work hours? What are the expectations around taking regular breaks and holidays throughout the year? Does your executive team model these expectations? What cultural messages are you giving to yourselves and your people around priorities?

- **Skill up your leaders on basic key organisational skills, such as prioritising, time management and delegation.** I'm amazed at how many emerging, mid-level (and even some senior) executives are still in the dark on the key steps to successful delegation. Many leaders inadvertently create overwork due to a lack of skill in these leadership fundamentals. It's not enough to thrust your first-time leaders into roles without giving them the tools to do it effectively. Teaching them fundamental time-management, delegation and prioritisation skills will not only assist them to be more effective in their roles (and avoid burnout), it will also reduce the chances that they inadvertently overwork their teams.
- **Review your organisational systems for red tape and bureaucracy—**those weeds that are

a small, but cumulative burden on people doing their job. Global burnout expert Christina Maslach refers to these as 'pebbles'—the tiny, incremental, yet irritating and painful stuff at work that can wear you down. Don't do this red-tape review in isolation, but instead ask your employees to name their biggest pebbles, so that you can see themes and patterns emerging around pain points. Do your systems and processes add extra burden to getting things done in your organisation, or are they streamlined to assist flow? Where do things get bogged down? Where are the choke points or areas of frustration? Fight intrusive regulations that do not add value.

- **Involve your employees in the what, the how and most definitely the why of their work.** Research has shown us that the more people feel involved in the creation of something—and, perhaps even more so *how* they need to do it, rather than purely being told *what* to do—the better they perform and the more engaged they will be. As well as reducing the chances of burnout, it also makes better business sense. 3M's most lucrative and famous product, the Post-it Note, was the result of allowing employees to spend 15 per cent of their time on projects of their choice.

—It might seem like a simple solution, to give employees more control over their work or projects. However, the reality of achieving this often requires a change in culture, systems and processes, as well as individual managers being willing to let go of the reins a little. A concerted effort across all of these fronts is required if you want to empower your employees to have some control over how their work is done.

- **Instigate organisation-wide monthly one-on-ones** between each manager and their direct report. I've written extensively on my leadership blog, The Leader's Digest, about the benefits of one-on-ones. These range from increased productivity, engagement and performance to increased trust between a manager and their direct report (provided they're done correctly!). You can check out a useful one-on-one template and more information on monthly one-on-ones in Appendix D. In the realm of reducing burnout, monthly one-on-ones decrease burnout by 39 per cent and having them weekly leads to a 47 per cent decrease in the odds of burnout, according to the 2020 Global Culture Report by O.C. Tanner. This is because they help with not only the *organise* strategy (discussing priorities, workload and issues) but also the *socialise* strategy (connection with your direct manager).

WHAT LEADERS CAN DO TO ORGANISE

- **Identify your team's strengths, and focus on enabling people to work from them.** Research has shown that when people work from their strengths, it not only gives them a greater sense of control over their work, but also leads to higher engagement, productivity and performance. Work with each of your direct reports to uncover their unique strengths—what they are good at and what they enjoy doing—and then consider how they can use these strengths more in their role and within the team. Then get your team together and share and discuss their individual and collective strengths. When I have worked with leadership teams on this exercise, they have reported not only a greater sense of trust and connection within the team, but also improved effectiveness and results for the whole team. See Appendix E on how you might go about this.

- **Explain clearly the outcomes, context and boundaries of the tasks you set for others, as well as giving out the task itself.** There's no need to micromanage. In fact, that is something you want to avoid. But *do* get clear on what success looks like when you give out a task or project. Provide the context of why it's important and where it fits into the bigger picture. When people understand how what they do links to the end result or broader goals, it makes it more meaningful for them. It also leads to fewer mistakes and misunderstandings.

—Incorporate coaching conversations into task assignments. What does success look like in this scenario? How will we know we have succeeded? What will we be seeing? What might be some potential obstacles? How long does each type of project that they are responsible for take? Why? How is their time getting allocated? What roadblocks are they running into? Explore necessary authorities to make decisions and what resources are required to complete the task. A little thought and purposeful attention at the beginning of a task-or project-assignment makes a big difference, to not only burnout

prevention, but also task or project success.
- Regardless of whether the organisation is doing this well at a macro level, you can still **do your part to involve your team members in the what, the how and most definitely the why of their work.** Spend time exploring with your direct reports how what they do fits into the bigger picture and makes a positive difference. Ask them regularly how you can both improve the way they approach their work. What do they see as being some opportunities for improvement in the 'how'? After all, they're the one doing it. It's likely they will have a better grasp of this than Mary in the HR department. We know that the more people feel involved in the creation of something—in other words, they are given context and purpose rather than just being told 'do this'—the better they perform and the more engaged they'll be. When leaders help employees feel a sense of purpose in their individual roles,

there is a 49 per cent reduction in burnout.
- **Ensure you are well-skilled in how to delegate and prioritise.** Two known accelerants of burnout are conflicting requests and ambiguity. Something as simple as following appropriate steps when delegating, and talking to peers and other relevant stakeholders about what else your team has on their plate, can help reduce these two things. See Appendix I for further tips on how to delegate effectively.
- **Keep your team aware of what projects are in the pipeline.** Knowing what might be coming up for your team will help both them—and you—plan and prepare. Regularly share with your team what's top of mind for *you* right now—what are *your* priorities? What are *your* direct manager's priorities? What are this team's and the organisation's top priorities? Take every opportunity you can to communicate these priorities and how what your team is doing is helping to achieve these. Keep your

team apprised of projects in the pipeline so they can consider how they could contribute to them.

- **Ask 'What should we ditch or delay?'** One of the most powerful questions a leader can ask themselves or their team is 'What do we need to *stop* doing?' Regularly assess with your direct manager, your peers and your own team what you can *take out* of the work funnel that is not helping you move towards the key collective goals. We tend to be very good at adding to our to-do list. But the most effective leaders are even better at subtracting from it or saying no to what's not essential. Encourage your team members to negotiate when it comes to tasks (see the next point for tips on this).
- **Use two-way communication around delegating new projects or tasks.** Instead of just assigning new responsibilities to employees without discussion, check in with them on their current workload and capacity first. If the new demands seem too extensive, work with them

to come up with some possible solutions. As much as possible, bring their input into deadlines, rather than simply assigning them autocratically. If the deadline is immovable, discuss their workload, including what might be able to be reprioritised on their list, or consider with them where and how they might get support. Encourage employees to speak up if they feel uncomfortable or need to renegotiate a deadline. However, remind them that it's better to do this at the beginning of the task allocation rather than at the last minute!

- **Watch the tendency to overload your top performers.** It's well known that we tend to do this—after all, if you want to get something done, it's common to give it to someone you can rely on to get the work done well. However, as we have covered earlier in the book, piling it all on our top performers can lead to overwork, a key contributor of burnout.

—If you have done some work identifying the respective strengths of your team, then you may be best to pause and be a bit more thoughtful about where, whom and why you might delegate certain tasks to certain people. Is there someone for whom this project might play to a strength of theirs, or offer a development opportunity? If you do have to give projects to your top performers, make sure you are having conversations about their current workload, like I've suggested in the previous point.
- **Ensure your performance rating system doesn't overly recognise working long hours.** Often managers will use the amount of time spent at work as one of the definers of superior performance, when there may be no correlation between the two. Ensure you evaluate the quality of your team members' efforts, not the quantity. The team generally knows who is doing quality work—and if they see recognition directed to 'quantity' rather than 'quality', it will

inevitably undermine their engagement.

WHAT INDIVIDUALS CAN DO TO ORGANISE

Although individual employees might have less power when it comes to how work is organised than their leaders do (and than the organisation as a whole), employees are not entirely at the mercy of the powers that be. There's no doubt that how you organise and prioritise your own workload can have an impact on your stress levels, as well as your performance.

Learning to prioritise and manage your time is an advisable skill for any employee to master, no matter what field you work in. And doing so effectively can reduce your chances of burnout. Here are some tips on how to do this:

- **Upskill yourself on time-management and prioritising skills.** These are vital for any worker, regardless of industry. Learning how to tackle your work more effectively and manage your time is a life skill. Applying a simple model such as the Time Management Matrix (see Appendix F)—which helps you decide on and prioritise tasks by urgency and importance, sorting out less urgent and important tasks that you should either delegate or not do at all—is one such example. Buying a book or taking a course on time management and prioritisation is another small step you can take towards taking back control of your workflow. One of the best books on this topic in my opinion is *Essentialism: The Disciplined Pursuit of Less,* by Greg McKeown. There are as many ways to get better at prioritising as there are to-dos on your long list of to-dos! Learning how to better manage your time and prioritise what's important will help you lower any negative stress and make you feel more in control of your work. Ask your employer about how they might support you in a way that makes sense both for them and for you.

- **Make a habit of discussing your priorities with your direct manager on a regular basis.** When I first became a people leader, I loved it when my direct reports would do this. Often I was unaware of what they already had on their plate, and a discussion of what was important and a priority from both of our perspectives was super useful for both of us. Sometimes, it was a simple reshuffling or confirmation of what they should be spending their time and effort on first. And at other times, we would discover that I had piled on extra tasks without knowing what else was going on or without giving them the necessary resources to succeed. This was a far better discussion to have at the beginning of the process than it was at a later stage when they were stressed and I was frustrated at lack of progress or subpar outcomes!
    —If you find yourself facing conflicting priorities or feeling overloaded, it's better to check in

with your boss than soldier on and come unstuck or get burned out later on. Come to your discussion with your direct manager prepared with some options and solutions for you both to discuss, not just the issue or problem itself—that's moving into whiny, complaining territory. Not only will this approach save time and provide you with some potential input into solving the problem, but it also shows initiative.

Here are some useful starters to have this type of conversation with your boss (adapt these to suit your own style or vernacular).

On prioritisation of too many tasks: 'Here is a list of what I currently have on, and a rough estimate of times (due dates, time taken). I'm concerned about getting through it given the addition of x (insert new task). Can we possibly have a discussion about how to best approach these in terms of resources and priorities? Which ones are the top three priorities this week/month/today?'

On how to negotiate workload: 'Here is what I currently have listed as my top priorities for the next week/month. I'm wondering ... given we are now looking at X as well (insert new task), it would be great to see where this new piece of work fits in with current priorities. What might we delay or push down on this list to accommodate this new project/task? Or what extra resources might be made available so that we can still do x whilst doing y?'

- **Evaluate what's on your plate regularly without it sneaking up on you.** If you're feeling overwhelmed by work demands, or a 'too full' plate seems to creep up on you on a regular basis, a purposeful review can help. You are then in a better position to negotiate priorities with your manager. A once-a-week and once-a-month check-in of what's on your plate and your top priorities, combined with setting out realistic time to complete these, is one simple way you can do this. It doesn't have to be convoluted or complex.

KEY TAKEOUTS

- Of all the 'burnout busters', the strategy of *organise*, which encapsulates one of the most pivotal organisational skills, prioritisation, perhaps packs the biggest punch of all when it comes to preventing burnout.
- A culture of overwork, a bias for action over reflection and trying to do too much all at once without the resources to do it are unfortunately prominent in society, organisations and individuals.
- The *organise* strategy goes a long way to combat these problems and can be applied at macro and micro levels within an organisation.
- Prioritisation, delegation, providing context to work and involving people in the 'how' of their work are key components of the *organise* strategy.

But let's say all this talk of the four-ise strategies has come a bit too late in the game. Maybe you suspect you, or someone you lead, may be suffering from burnout. In the next two chapters, I will delve into some actions you can take if this is the case. You might not read both chapters—just opting for the one most relevant to you—but they are a useful guide to dip into if the burnout bug has already bitten.

CHAPTER 11

SO YOU THINK YOU MIGHT HAVE BURNOUT – NOW WHAT?

'HR were really good at trying to help me get a return-to-work programme, and so was talking to my manager. We then went and met with Occupational Health. And as a part of that, I had to have an assessment—a sort of psychological assessment for work practices—and that was really good, to talk to him. They wanted me to cut my hours right back or even consider leaving, and I said, "No, that's not what I want."'

Margaret, professional who experienced burnout

If you've come this far in the book you might be saying to yourself quietly,

'Crikey, I think I can tick waaay too many of those boxes in the Recognise chapter ... More than I'd care to admit!' If that's you, you may be on the burnout on-ramp.

This is good news. Well, it's not good news that you might be suffering from burnout—that sucks. But the good news is that you've employed one of the first strategies to give burnout the bird. You've recognised it. And, as we now know, recognising the signs of burnout is the first step to being able to do something about it. You can't address something if you're in the dark about it.

Although there are always going to be things beyond your control and that may be contributing to your burnout, there are also always things which *are* within your control and that you *can* do to address it.

It may be that you work in an organisation that has a great culture of supporting mental wellbeing, and you can lean into that. If that's the case, then brilliant, use it. If that's not the case, take heart—all is not lost. This chapter gives you some first steps that you can follow if you think you might be suffering from burnout, regardless of where your organisation is in its mental wellbeing journey.

1. PRACTISE SELF-COMPASSION

Kick those self-critical voices into touch (at least for the moment).

This one is a tricky one for me to suggest with my coach hat on. I'm not proposing you avoid self-reflection—self-awareness and taking responsibility for your part in any given situation is always a worthwhile pursuit. You may have done some things to contribute to your burnout. But, let's remember, burnout is rarely (or never) entirely the burned-out person's fault. Beating yourself up or falling into the trap of thinking you're somehow weak or flawed for experiencing burnout is not useful. Nor is it true. The research unequivocally tells us so.

When I burned out, I fell into the grip of the self-blame game. It just made my situation worse. When I started to take some advice from friends and loved ones on how to be a bit kinder to myself, it heralded the start of my climb out of it.

One simple way to bring self-compassion into the picture at this point is to treat yourself as you would a dear friend. What advice would you give to them if they were in your situation? What words or guidance might you offer that friend? Say these things to yourself. Often we speak to ourselves in a harsh and judgemental way that we would never use in speaking to others. So, take some of your own wise and kind instruction that you would offer to a friend.

Another way to practise self-compassion is to compare yourself to others but, in this instance, in a helpful, positive way. Remind yourself of all the high-achieving people I've listed in this book who have experienced burnout. They certainly weren't losers by any stretch of the imagination. In fact, many of them were at the highest levels within their profession—'super achievers', even. There may also be people you admire in your field who have also suffered from burnout. (Take another look at the chapter 'Who is most at risk of burnout?'.)

Remember, you're not alone in suffering from burnout. And there is no shame in admitting that.

2. REACH OUT—DON'T TRY TO FIGHT BURNOUT ON YOUR OWN

From a practical perspective, it might be worth getting in touch with your doctor or another health professional. They can offer some practical support and advice upfront.

If you can, and if it feels safe to do so, speak to your direct manager about how you're feeling. Practise how you might go about this in a way that comes across professionally. If you have a trusting relationship with your boss, it's likely they will want to support you in getting from exhausted and overwhelmed to feeling engaged and on top again. However, they certainly can't help if they don't know what's going on with you.

If that doesn't feel safe, can you get in contact with someone from HR, if you have that function in your organisation? Or is there a trusted colleague at work—someone who can act as an objective, confidential sounding board that you can speak to about what you're experiencing? Even a former boss or mentor who you trust, or whose judgement you respect, might be able to offer a listening ear and provide some ideas on a way forward.

Maybe you could speak to a loved one or a friend outside of work, or even take up the opportunity to use those mental-health services that most organisations offer, such as EAP. Remember, these services are confidential and anonymous.

The main thing is to try not to fight burnout on your own. I remember when I was feeling burned out—I just didn't have the capacity to think straight, nor the energy to see beyond the next report I had to write. I definitely did not have the ability to see objectively what I could do next. For me, help came when I opened up to my supportive boss, my supportive husband (he was the bomb, even though he couldn't quite understand what was going on with me) and my close friends, who showed up and told me—kindly, but in no uncertain terms—that things had to change.

3. WORK WITHIN YOUR CIRCLE OF CONTROL

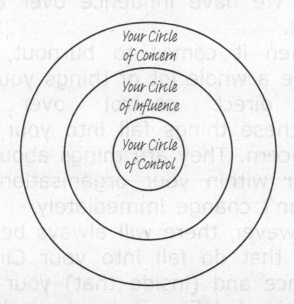

As Stephen Covey outlined in *The 7 Habits of Highly Effective People*, there are two main areas on which you can spend your energy—your Circle of Concern and your Circle of Influence. According to Covey, highly effective people spend *far* more energy focusing on their Circle of Influence (things they can do something about) than on their Circle of Concern (the things in their life that concern them). In a nutshell, the main point of the model is that instead of doing a lot of teeth-gnashing over things that simply concern us that we can't do anything about, we should spend our time and energy on the things we have influence over or can control.

When it comes to burnout, there may be a whole lot of things you don't have direct control over right now—these things fall into your Circle of Concern. They are things about your job, or within your organisation, that you can't change immediately.

However, there will always be some things that do fall into your Circle of Influence and (inside that) your Circle of Control. So, ask yourself the following:
- What *is* within my influence and control in this situation?
- What small, proactive or positive things can I do to respond?

Brainstorm (maybe with a trusted and supportive friend or colleague) as many things as you can think of, big or small, which you could do that might help you move out of burnout. These may fall into the 'What could I do in the immediate and short term?' camp, as well as the 'What could I do in the longer term?' category. Both are helpful and valid. Make the list as long and as creative as you can. Then go back over that list and choose the ones that seem the most practical or useful to start with.

Caveat: when it comes to any big decision, like 'Should I leave my job or profession?', hold off from deciding that for a wee while. Instead, sit with the options and don't make any rash decisions. Let it percolate. We rarely make the best decisions in our lives from a heightened (or depleted) emotional state. But there may be a couple of small steps you could take, right now, that may ease the load, make things a little lighter and easier to bear and give you some respite.

4. REALISE THAT RECOVERING FROM

BURNOUT WON'T HAPPEN OVERNIGHT—BUT IT WILL HAPPEN

I'm going to channel Rachel Hunter and her Pantene ad from the '90s for a minute, where she swishes her hair and promises us, 'It won't happen overnight, but it will happen.' Burnout is not glamorous like Rachel's hair, but the principle is the same. Just like burnout doesn't happen overnight, it won't get solved overnight either.

Burnout doesn't go away on its own. And it certainly won't go away unless you address the underlying issues causing it. Whatever you do, don't ignore burnout and think that if you just dig deeper into your already depleted reserves and soldier on, it's going to help, or that you'll endure and get through it. Putting your head in the sand and changing nothing is a sure-fire tactic to take you further down the burnout road. It will cause more damage, too—potentially to your career, your health and your personal relationships.

Recovery from burnout is a slow journey. It's not like a sprint to some imaginary finish line. You'll need to align your expectations to the fact that it will take some time and space to get back into that flourishing and positive state you yearn for.

5. IDENTIFY THE WHY

Exploring and reflecting on the root causes of your burnout helps you get to the why—the nub of the issue. That way, you'll be better positioned to tackle it in the most effective way. It also helps you to prioritise where you first can take some action.

For starters, you might want to take another look at the 'What causes burnout?' chapter and see which of these factors are resonating for you, and how, specifically, they are showing up in your work. There are a couple of resources in the appendices, such as the stress diary, to help you do that.

Take some time to examine the negative feelings you currently have about your role. Once you've done this and some of the exercises in the appendices, you will likely then be in a better position to think of ideas and ways you might be able to reduce or eliminate that source of stress. Doing this shifts your energy from that of helpless victim to someone who has both some control and potential solutions.

6. MAKE REFUELLING AND RELAXATION YOUR TOP PRIORITY

As hard as it may seem to do, you need to make yourself your top priority for a bit. If this seems too much of a reach or a selfish thing to do, consider this: how are you showing up for your loved ones, colleagues and other important stakeholders in the state you're in now? It's pretty difficult to be your best for anyone when you're burned out. So, if it helps to think of it this way, put yourself first *for them.* This might be an approach that's easier for you to swallow. It doesn't matter what your logic or rationale is for doing this, but do it you must.

Make time for relaxation and for doing nothing at all. Yes, I get it—most of us have busy lives filled to the brim with big responsibilities, both inside and outside of work. Taking off for a holiday to some tropical island is outside the realm of what's possible for most of us at the best of times, let alone in times impacted by Covid-19. But there may be things that you're currently committed to that are draining the life out of you, and that you *can* temporarily say no to. Your job is to find more space in your life right now.

In this space, seek joy. Find little things each day or week that might bring you happiness and allow you to relax. A walk in nature. Curling up with a blanket and a good book. That cup of coffee from your favourite café to drink outside your workplace in the park down the road for ten minutes. Meeting with a friend who fills up your tank. Seek out little things that bring you joy.

Whatever it is that is a pause, a stop, a metaphorical (or literal) slow deep breath that lifts your spirits will help to fill up your tank. Ensure you find at least a few minutes each day to wind down and do nothing but 'be', or get lost in the moment. Do something with no purpose at all other than to enjoy or relax.

7. PUT WORK IN ITS PLACE

This can be hard, especially when our identity is so strongly tied up with what we do professionally. But that overused quote that we will never lie on our death beds wishing we had spent more time at work is overused for a reason. *It's true.*

What are the most important things in your life? Write these down and put them in order of importance. Does your current calendar reflect that list? Maybe the balance of what you're focusing on in your life has got a bit skew-whiff.

Take a look at the Wheel of Life exercise in Appendix K, which I borrowed from Jayne Chater, author of *A Slight Detour: How to Successfully Navigate Your Family and Career,* as a simple way to review the balance and focus in your life. If health, family, children and friends are the most important things to you, what small tweak could you muster to move towards honouring those more? When we live in alignment with what we value most in our lives, then this fills up our tank and ... well, we feel more aligned. I'm guessing that if you're burned out, this alignment is a bit out of whack.

You don't have to make grand, sweeping gestures. Small and sustainable nudges in the right direction can help you get the balance back and put work in its place.

8. SPRING CLEAN YOUR COMMITMENTS

Evaluate your existing commitments and consider cancelling or rescheduling a few. Get rid of those energy vampires and commitments that you feel you 'should do' but which really drain you. Or, to put this another way, say 'no' unless it's a 'hell yes!' Consider slowing down your life outside of work for a little while. Reduce stressors in your life where you can. It won't be forever, but it may help you get some of the space you need to recover from burnout.

9. TAKE A BREAK

You may not be able to take a big holiday. But is a long weekend where you do nothing but recuperate and relax off the cards? Taking a break on its own won't solve burnout, but any break may give you some space to consider what you need to do next.

10. RECOGNISE THE MIND–BODY CONNECTION

Research shows that the body and mind are inextricably linked. When your body is fit and healthy, and when you employ some straightforward interventions to incorporate physical health, your ability to perform and remain resilient at work is dramatically increased.

10.1 EXERCISE

When you're burned out, the thought of going to the gym and doing a major workout may seem like just another overwhelming thing to do on your already overwhelming to-do list. But some form of exercise is crucial to help you get back to where you need to be. Even a daily short walk in nature has been shown to have positive effects on mood, energy levels and cognitive function.

If you are committed to exercise already, keep it up, but make sure you have some relaxing, lower-energy exercise in there, like yoga, golf or walking, as well as hitting the gym and going hard-out. As Dr Libby Weaver, author of many books on this subject including *The Invisible Load: A Guide to Overcoming Stress and Overwhelm* has warned, 'Too much high-intensity exercise ... can trigger our stress response.' So make sure your schedule includes some lower-intensity, relaxing exercise as well as that F45 class you dig so much.

If you can't remember the last time you donned your trainers and broke a sweat, then just start with something small, like a daily walk in the park. But build it into your daily routine, making exercise one of the most important things you do each day. You've heard this before, but when you're burned out, it becomes even more important than ever.

10.2 PRACTISE MINDFULNESS

I discovered the power of meditation and mindfulness when I first became burned out. Along with exercise, it helped me enormously. It still does. Mindfulness-based stress reduction and other mindfulness programmes have been shown to reduce burnout, so get meditating. It doesn't have to be all kumbaya or hippy-dippy. Mindfulness and meditation have taken their rightful place in mainstream science as a stress-reducing superpower.

There are so many meditation apps around. My go-to is Headspace, but do some research and find one that works for you. Even just five to ten minutes a day is all you need to see some positive effects. Once again, a daily walk or practising meditation isn't going to fully cure burnout—nor is the reason that you are burned out the fact that you weren't doing these things. But if you *are* burned out, they can certainly help your recovery.

11. UP YOUR PRIORITISING AND TIME-MANAGEMENT SKILLS

Now's the time to look at your time-management practices. This won't solve burnout if the cause of your burnout is overwork, but it might help you manage your workload a bit better and find some space to slow down for a few moments. It's also something that's within your control.

Maybe you've already been on a time-management course previously but have let bad habits take over? Here are some simple yet effective strategies to remind you:

- Write a daily and weekly to-do list using something like the Time Management Matrix, which is explained in Appendix F. Rank your tasks according to importance or urgency to plan your day and focus your mind.

- The 80/20 rule applies to workload as much as it does to many other things. Eighty per cent of our work contributes to less than 20 per cent of its value. What do you see as currently the most crucial 20 per cent of your workload? Write this down. What can you do to concentrate more on this?
- Is there anything in your work that you can ditch, delay or delegate? Overwork and a feeling of being overcome by work commitments are often caused by overloading our diaries with things that don't matter. For the next week or month, look at your diary and activities closely. What can you take out that is not helping you get ahead on your priorities or that key 20 per cent?
- Manage your inbox (rather than letting it manage you). Set times of the day to check your email rather than constantly checking it as it arrives. Batch times at the beginning and end of the day (and maybe at lunchtime, if you really have to) to check email. Let your

stakeholders know you only check emails once or twice a day, and that if it's urgent to phone or text you. What are the times you will clear your inbox daily?
- Limit distractions. When you time block for a certain activity, turn off all notifications, beeps and anything else that will take you away from concentrating on the *one thing* that's in front of you. Research has shown us that multitasking is not only a myth, it's actually really bad for productivity. It also stops us from practising mindfulness (being present, in the moment, non-judgementally). And as I mentioned above, practising mindfulness not only reduces stress and increases our decision-making capability, it also leads us to be more productive. What can you do to limit distractions?

12. LEARN HOW TO SAY NO AND SET BOUNDARIES

(BUT NOT IN A CAREER-LIMITING WAY)

Saying 'no' can be challenging, but it's an important skill to master at work. It also might help you prevent burnout. It becomes even more important when you're suffering from it.

It can feel especially difficult (and risky) when you're saying 'no' to someone in a more powerful position (such as your boss). I get it. But knowing *when* and *how* to say 'no' is an essential skill when it comes to thriving and being effective at work.

Here are my four ways to help you get better at saying 'no' at work:

- Ascertain the importance of the task with the person who has asked you to do it. Before jumping in with a response, think about how important the request for your time and energy is on the 'scale of priorities'. Ask yourself the following questions:
    —How integral is this task in helping to achieve my/our priorities?
    —Is this going to help move me/us closer to achieving our goals

or strategy? Or is it a 'nice-to-have' that has the 'feel-good' factor but drags me away from what needs to be done?
- If saying 'no' straight off is too hard, buy yourself some time so that you can consider it further, or ask more clarifying questions around time commitments and priorities. A simple 'let me think about it and get back to you' can work.

—Eliminate something else. If the task is of integral importance, then something else will need to go. Try saying something like, 'I'm currently working on project X and Y. However, if you feel this new project is more important, are you comfortable with me prioritising this over the others or would you prefer we consider other alternatives such as assigning this work to someone else?'

—Communicate the fact you *can* do it now, but make sure you discuss what *cannot* be done at this time as a consequence—or what could instead be delegated to someone else.

—Letting go of something from the priorities list will help to reduce the likelihood of increased stress levels, errors and producing unsatisfactory results.
- If it has to be a 'yes', ask for a due date. It seems obvious, but one of the mistakes I've made before is creating my own artificial deadlines. Rather than saying, 'I'll have that done by...', instead ask, 'When do you need this by?' On occasions where I have imposed my own somewhat unrealistic deadlines, that I've then struggled to meet, I've found that if I had simply asked, I could have bought myself a few more days—and a whole lot less stress.

The art of saying 'no' takes time to fine-tune, and the first time we do it can seem awkward. But learning to set boundaries and negotiate your workload helps a ton. For more on how to do this, check out Greg McKeown's book *Essentialism*, which I mentioned earlier.

REMEMBER, THERE'S HOPE...

If you're suffering from burnout, perhaps the most encouraging thing is to know that you can recover, and you don't necessarily need to leave your job or profession to do so. I will leave you with the following quote from someone we interviewed for this book, who experienced burnout and recovered—going on to find the passion and engagement she had lost when she was burned out:

'I am more efficient. I am enjoying work—the time I spend with my patients, I'm really connecting with them a lot better. I guess I've always enjoyed it, but there's always been some other underlying thing when I was experiencing burnout, that sort of sense of unease or something.

'I am communicating so much better with my colleagues and with management now. I can sit down, and I can think. I think I'm better than I was before. Whether or not

that's to do with time and experience too, I'm not sure. I am better than ever.

'And I was just thinking this morning—because it's now been eleven years since I've been a consultant, and five of those have been so hard—and I thought, "Imagine what I can do in the next ten! I can't wait!" Yeah, I'm really excited about it.'

Jenny, surgeon

KEY TAKEOUTS:

- Practise self-compassion. Beating yourself up is not helpful, and burnout is rarely entirely (or even mostly) the individual's fault.
- Reach out—don't try to fight burnout on your own.
- Work within your circle of control. What small things are within your power to make positive changes in your work environment? There is always something you *can* do.
- Burnout doesn't happen overnight, just as it doesn't disappear

overnight. But you can and will recover.

- Identify the 'why?' and the root cause of your burnout.
- Make refuelling and relaxing your top priority.
- Focusing on other parts of your life that are just as (or more) important can help you shift focus.
- Spring-clean your commitments.
- Take a break—even a small one will help.
- Recognise the mind–body connection through things like exercise and practising mindfulness.
- Up your prioritising and time-management skills.
- Learn how to say no and set boundaries (but not in a career-limiting way).
- Remember, there's hope. You can and will recover from burnout if you take some positive steps.

CHAPTER 12

I'M LEADING SOMEONE WHO I SUSPECT MIGHT BE BURNED OUT – NOW WHAT?

'We rise by lifting others.'
American writer Robert Ingersoll

Before you do anything, consider these things...

The first thing you need to understand is that many people won't feel comfortable coming to their boss if they think they're suffering from burnout. In fact, they may even go so far as to try to hide it from you. We know this from both the research conducted here in New Zealand through the Cogo Workplace Wellbeing Survey 2020 and a multitude of studies overseas. In my role as an executive coach, I've also personally seen people's reticence to put their hand up and open up to their direct manager when they're struggling. As we've discussed, there's still stigma attached to burnout. Many employees don't want to be seen as not keeping up with their job requirements.

Secondly, like myself and many others who I've spoken to who have suffered from burnout, we may not even recognise the signs or symptoms in ourselves at first. It's possible that you and/or their colleagues may be noticing things that the person suffering from burnout isn't. As Jenny, a professional suffering from burnout, admitted earlier in the book: 'My colleagues knew that I wasn't right for a long time ... I didn't identify it myself, but other people could see it.' This is an important backdrop and context to consider before you take any steps to support someone you suspect may be suffering from burnout.

I'm hoping that before you do anything, you've put effort into building a trusting and respectful relationship with your direct report. This is key to any successful working relationship and to a high-performance team. Low trust is poison to positive working relationships. If there's no (or low) trust between the two of you, it will make it very difficult for you to support them directly, so building trust should be your first priority. (Actually, that should be your first priority at any time in your role as a leader—not just when you suspect burnout may be lurking near someone you lead.)

IS IT BURNOUT?

You may not even be 100 per cent sure this person is suffering from burnout. Hold that assumption lightly. It may well be burnout, but their behaviour and performance could also be affected by other things, such as tough personal circumstances. This is why the first step is always creating a trusting environment so that they are comfortable opening up and sharing with you what's going on.

Perhaps you've seen this person demonstrating some of the key signs of burnout: chronic exhaustion, increased cynicism, withdrawal or increased depersonalisation in their work, or reduced professional efficacy. Maybe their reduced sense of performance is real; they aren't performing to their usual standard and you are actually seeing a slip in their work.

As we know from reading this book, if they're displaying *all three* of these symptoms (and haven't always acted in this way), this is a warning sign of burnout. Ask yourself:
- Is this how this employee typically behaves, or does it seem out of character?
- Has their performance slipped, when previously they were engaged and performing?

Watch out that you don't fall prey to the fundamental attribution error, where we tend to over-emphasise dispositional or personality-based explanations for behaviours while under-emphasising situational explanations. That means, we often jump to the conclusion that any non-performance or a drop in motivation or engagement is due to some fault of the person—laziness or not being on their game, for instance. If they're demonstrating those three signs, however, *burnout is a likely cause of their behaviour.* And if that's the case, it's more likely to do with the work or work environment, than them as a person.

Your job is to first seek to understand the root causes of the behaviours you're seeing. Keep an open mind at this early stage. After all, you don't have all the facts.

Even if you aren't sure, but you sense this person is struggling in some way, it's really important that you don't leave them unsupported. *Don't do nothing.* A skilled leader will gently and sensitively check things out. It may take a few conversations or gentle nudges, so be patient. Don't be disheartened or get put off if at first you get a 'nope, everything's fine' response.

Now, let's say you have a solid level of trust and respect. You've done some reflection on the situation as you see it. You're ready, with an open, curious mind. And you've started to see some of the red flags or symptoms of burnout in this person you lead. The next step is raising it with them ...

HAVE A CONVERSATION

The first thing to do is to have a private, unrushed conversation with the person. You can begin by sharing with them what you're noticing. This is a kind of gentle feedback conversation, so all the principles of effective feedback apply here, too: be as specific as you can (with examples, if possible) about what behaviour or patterns you've been noticing. Make sure it's a two-way conversation, not a monologue on your part. Pause and give them time to respond. Seek their feedback with open questions. Work to create psychological trust in the conversation.

Alternatively, you can simply ask, 'How are you going? I know there's a lot going on right now and we've been under a lot of pressure lately (or insert what context is right here), and I wanted to check in with how that's affecting you, especially from a wellbeing perspective ... I care about you as a team mate and I'm just wondering about your wellbeing at the moment...?' You get the gist.

The key is to show support and concern, as opposed to making it an inquisition. This isn't the time for a heavy-duty, non-performance conversation. Be compassionate, not punitive.

In this initial conversation, do lots of active listening, demonstrate supportive body language and use lots of open, curious questions to understand where they're at. Paraphrase back to them what you think you're hearing. Avoid defensiveness, and refrain from jumping into 'solution mode' too early. It's important you *both* explore what's happening, so that you *both* increase your understanding. You may not even necessarily agree with everything they are saying, but people first want to feel heard and understood, before they're ready to listen to what you have to say. Simply allowing space to listen to your direct report can be a powerful first step in supporting them to address burnout.

Even if they admit they are overwhelmed or struggling, they may not label it as burnout—and that's OK. The key is to let them know that you support them and want to help. You may even give them this book and suggest they self-assess by going through the checklists in the 'Recognise' chapter—they may then be able to recognise the symptoms in themselves.

Practise empathy. Give the person positive reinforcement and positive, genuine feedback. Remind them of any good work they are doing or any highlights in their work that you have seen.

Importantly, be super aware of confidentiality and any of your organisation's HR protocols that you may need to follow with conversations like these.

This initial approach is unlikely to be a one-off conversation but the first of a series of meaningful conversations over time. The aim is to raise their awareness of what you've been seeing and, together, work out a plan forward.

FIND A WAY FORWARD, TOGETHER

Once you're both on the same page and agree that they might be suffering from burnout, then you can move into action. But remember, one of the main causes of burnout is a feeling of a lack of control over their work. So don't fall into the trap of reinforcing that here. A dictatorial approach, where *you* decide what's going to happen, is less helpful than some form of co-creation on what to do next.

Talk collaboratively about what's possible within the confines of their work, the organisation and what needs to be delivered. Your goal is to work towards positive outcomes for all three key stakeholders—them, you and the organisation. It might mean changing expectations in the short term. It might mean some compromises. Work with them to see what the best solutions and fixes are.

Return to the four '-ise' strategies and see where you can apply them here. Remember, they are *recognise, destigmatise, socialise* and *organise*. Which strategies from those chapters might help this person now?

You might also want to ask them if there is anything that you're doing that might be contributing to the problem.

Won't this be a bit confronting? Yes. But seeking honest, open feedback from those you lead on how you can lead them better is something all good leaders do. Make sure to thank them for their feedback, seek to understand further and don't be defensive or make them feel that giving you an honest answer is a career-limiting move.

SOME PRACTICAL IDEAS FOR ACTIONS

Once you've had these initial conversations, here are some options for actions you can take. You'll need to work out what's possible or suitable given the unique circumstances of the individual, the situation, and your organisational culture and work requirements.

- Ask them, 'What would help right now?' Brainstorm a number of options together—don't stop at too few. Then have another look to see which ones are both possible and practical. Avoid the knee-jerk response of merely taking work off them. Instead, involve them and

give them a say and some control over strategies.
- Look at their workload together. Where are the pain points? Is there anything in the *Organise* chapter they, you or others can do that could reduce overwork? Are there small tweaks in the way they do their work that may help to reduce overwork or a lack of control?
- Prioritise. Look at their current work schedules and priorities together. Take the time to get super clear on their top three priorities. Is there anything in their workload they can ditch, delay or delegate?
- Redirecting some work temporarily may well be a solution, but it's a short-term one. Discuss how this might be done practically. This may give you both some space in the short term to work out longer-term solutions.
- Can they take a short break? This in itself won't be enough, but they may need to take a break from work initially to recharge their batteries and get in the right headspace to find a way forward.

If you decide to do this, remind them that there is no shame or negative repercussions attached to them taking this approach. Once they come back, instead of just welcoming them back to the same-old after their break, it will be necessary to put in support structures to address the root cause of their burnout.
- Is a change in work environment possible, even in a small way? Explore this.
- What can you do to increase meaningful social connection in a way that works for them? Are they feeling isolated at work? Increasing your one-on-ones and including a wellbeing element to these catch-ups is a good idea. Not only will it provide support, but it will also increase social connection with one of the most important people in their work life—you. Use this time to coach (see Appendix G for some great coaching questions), mentor and direct.
- Let them know what support the organisation can offer in these

situations. Remind them of services like EAP (Employee Assistance Programme). If you have used any of these support services yourself, you might even tell them what you found helpful. This will go a long way to destigmatising the use of these services.

- Keep reiterating that there is no shame in experiencing burnout (or any mental distress, for that matter). They need to hear this from you as their direct manager. Share your own experiences of stress, or burnout if you've experienced it, and maybe share what worked for you.
- Go in to bat for them (and your team) if there are some systemic issues that might be causing burnout. It may be that they are not the only one who is experiencing burnout. Remember that, as their direct manager, you have enormous influence in these areas.
- Keep checking in on them regularly and asking them how they are, to

show you care. Encourage them to work with what is in their control.

KEY TAKEOUTS

- The first priority of any leader should be to build trust. Focus on this first.
- If you suspect that someone you lead may be suffering from burnout, hold your assumptions lightly.
- Work with the person to raise awareness that they may be suffering from burnout, then tackle it together using some of the practical steps outlined in this chapter.

BEYOND BURNOUT – SUMMING IT ALL UP

Worldwide, burnout is a problem that's costing us a lot of money. Stress and burnout are costing the global economy over $500 billion USD a year. The World Health Organization came out in 2019 and named burnout an occupational phenomenon. This says a lot. It points to the growing and significant crisis that burnout is creating across the globe. And it's a growing phenomenon in New Zealand and Australia, too.

The costs of burnout to our workplaces are alarming—absenteeism, lost productivity, lower engagement and increased staff turnover are all by-products of burnout. This doesn't count the personal costs to individuals who are suffering from it. Burnout wreaks havoc on people's professional efficacy, performance, health and personal lives.

Burnout is the insidious, misunderstood and hidden malaise that's preventing our workplaces from being the places they have the potential to be.

And it's on the rise. Both globally, and in Australia and New Zealand, the burnout statistics are moving—and not in the right direction. It is a clear and growing threat to workplaces and employees alike. Early indications are that Covid-19 will exacerbate stress and burnout figures, but it's worth noting that many of the causes of burnout were present and prevalent in our workplaces already, without the added pressure of this pandemic.

It's time we changed that. Organisations, leaders and individuals alike can take steps to spot it, stop it and stamp it out.

WHAT EXACTLY IS BURNOUT?

Burnout is a state of emotional, physical and mental exhaustion caused by excessive and prolonged stress related to your professional life.

Stress is not burnout. Prolonged, chronic stress, however, can and does lead to burnout. So it's the *level* and the *duration* of the stress that's important here. Depression is also not burnout, although the two share similar symptoms and are linked. Extreme burnout has been shown to lead to depression in some cases.

MYTHS

Although burnout is a word that's bandied about within the halls of our workplaces, it's still largely misunderstood. And that doesn't help us address it effectively. Our mental models stop us from remedying it. These myths can cause increased damage to people experiencing burnout, as well as to their organisations. And these commonly held myths can prevent organisations from being effective in stamping out burnout.

First, there's the myth that burnout is mainly an individual's problem (and probably their fault). In fact, burnout is predominantly an organisational problem, not an individual one. Recognising this is key to how we tackle it.

Another myth is that people who suffer from burnout are weak, 'can't hack it' or are poor performers. Burnout can (and does) happen to anyone. In fact, research has shown that high performers can be more at risk of burnout. You can even have feelings of high engagement towards your work and profession—and, at the same time, be burned out.

Burnout isn't solved simply by going on holiday or taking a break from work. The root causes of burnout lie with the organisation. It's a bit like treating the sick fish, when it's the water that's contaminated. Pop that fish back into the water and it's likely to get sick again.

We also need to recognise that stress, in and of itself, is not bad. In fact, we need a certain amount of stress or pressure to bring about high performance and engagement. So we need to understand stress in a more nuanced way if we're to tackle burnout and stress-related issues in our workplaces.

And although overwork is a key cause of burnout, it's not the only one.

There are other factors which also play a significant role in the burnout biography. Likewise, working long hours isn't the be-all and end-all—long hours do not necessarily lead to burnout, although they can if it's the only way you can get the job done.

WHO IS MOST AT RISK FROM BURNOUT?

Anyone can suffer from burnout. Organisational factors play a much greater role in determining burnout rates than any individual factors do.

That said, certain personality traits play a small, but statistically relevant, role in whether you're more susceptible to burnout. For example, if you have perfectionistic tendencies, or have a Type A personality, you're slightly more at risk, according to the research. Traits like extroversion, self-efficacy and self-esteem also have an impact, according to studies.

The jury is still out on whether men or women suffer from burnout more. What does seem to be emerging in the research is that men and women demonstrate burnout in different ways, with men more often demonstrating cynicism and women exhibiting more signs of exhaustion. Both cynicism and exhaustion are two red flags of burnout. More research is needed to determine whether those from the LGBTQ community are more at risk. Given that isolation and a perceived lack of fairness are two significant drivers of burnout, I would suspect they are. I would be curious to see more research on this.

Certain professions and sectors feature more prominently in the burnout statistics. For example, those in the human services, medical, emergency work, teaching and legal professions are over-represented in burnout statistics compared with the general public. There's also an increasing spotlight on CEO and senior executive burnout, too.

At the same time, burnout is everywhere—across all industries, sectors, professions and levels within our workplaces. None of us is necessarily immune.

WHAT CAUSES BURNOUT?

There are six main causes of burnout. They are:
- overwork
- a lack of control
- insufficient rewards
- a sense of isolation
- the absence of fairness, and
- a values conflict between the individual and the organisation or team.

Any one of these factors can lead to burnout, but when more than one of these causes is present, it's likely to increase the chances of burnout occurring. These causes can also be interconnected. When they're intertwined, it creates a perfect burnout storm.

WHAT CAN WE DO TO SPOT IT, STOP IT AND STAMP IT OUT?

If when you were halfway through reading this book it all became a bit depressing and overwhelming, fear not!

As we covered, there are steps that organisations, leaders and individuals can take which can prevent burnout and create workplaces where people thrive, as opposed to burning out. In particular, leadership plays a significant role in doing this, whether that's from an organisational or individual perspective.

The four key strategies to safeguard us from burnout are *recognise, destigmatise, socialise* and *organise*. You can apply these four strategies whether you're an individual contributor in your organisation or the CEO.

RECOGNISE

The first thing we can do is learn to recognise the symptoms of burnout. Burnout can creep up on us—you don't wake up one day flourishing and then the next day find you're burned out. It's a slow creep. It's helpful to understand that there are three red flags or symptoms of burnout. They are:
- chronic exhaustion
- increased cynicism or depersonalisation, and
- reduced professional efficacy.

In the 'Recognise' chapter, we outlined these warning signs in more detail. However, the main point is that when we see a combination of all three of these signs in ourselves or our colleagues, it is likely to signal burnout. There are also surveys like the Maslach Burnout Inventory (which is outlined in Appendix L), that organisations can adopt to spot burnout trends within their organisation.

DESTIGMATISE

Like a lot of mental distress in the workplace, burnout is shrouded in stigma. Many who are suffering from burnout do not reach out for help but continue to battle burnout alone, for fear of negative consequences. It's vital that we start to talk more openly about mental wellbeing in our workplaces and make it safe for people to speak up.

Leaders play a big role in doing this. And the more senior you are in an organisation, the more impact you will have. From having more 'How are we going?' conversations alongside the 'What are we doing?' ones, to leaders having the courage to speak about their own challenges and approaches to stress or mental wellbeing, we can make it safer for others to do so, too.

Organisations and different professions must also look at their systems, processes and culture through this burnout and mental wellbeing lens. Are we making it psychologically safe for people to be open about burnout? Or are we inadvertently pushing people underground when it comes to this and other mental distress? We cannot address an issue effectively if it remains hidden.

SOCIALISE

Social isolation, either perceived or real, is a big cause of burnout. And according to the research, we're feeling lonelier at work than ever before. The third '-ise' to combatting burnout, socialise, is to be purposeful in creating opportunities for social connection in our workplaces. It's not enough to leave this to chance—or to individual employees. Again, leaders and organisations pack a bigger punch here, because they have greater power and influence over culture.

We learned in the 'Socialise' chapter that there are a number of ways you can encourage better and stronger social connection at work, whether that's from a macro, organisational level, or from an individual leadership or employee level. One of the most important aspects is to create trust. Trust between the employees and the organisation, trust between a direct manager and their direct report and trust within teams are all pivotal to the socialise strategy.

ORGANISE

When it comes to overwork, two big accelerants of burnout are conflicting requests and priorities—and ambiguity. How we organise and prioritise work plays an important role in safeguarding people from burnout. This involves things like involving people in the 'how' and the 'why' of their work, not just the 'what'. It also includes ensuring people are not charged with a task without the corresponding resources to do it. It means being crystal clear on priorities and not having too many of them!

Clarity of communication, and priorities, are key to the organise strategy for burnout. Once again, individuals can take charge in the way they organise their work and employ strategies for influencing and negotiating their workload with their managers to prevent burnout. But if leaders and those at the highest levels within a company can adopt the strategies outlined in the 'Organise' chapter, it's going to pack the biggest punch.

MOVING BEYOND BURNOUT...

Although the growing trend of burnout may be sobering, or if you have realised through reading this book the substantial costs of this insidious workplace affliction, we absolutely can take positive steps to spot it, stop it and stamp it out. The good news is that many of the strategies outlined in this book not only reduce burnout, they also improve outcomes in other areas within our organisations.

Now is the time to ensure that having both people and profits thriving are no longer mutually exclusive. In fact, if we take better care of our people, we will see better outcomes for all stakeholders.

We have looked at burnout here through a leadership lens and acknowledged that a lot of the work we need to do takes place at the organisational level. However, even if you are an individual contributor lower down in the hierarchy of your organisation, you too can have a positive impact by employing the strategies in this book.

You might also want to 'accidentally' leave this book lying around in the staffroom kitchen, or you could even consider buying it for someone you think may benefit from it!

We have an opportunity to move beyond burnout in our workplaces, to tackle this major problem in our organisations and together spot it, stop it and, perhaps in time, stamp it out.

APPENDIX A

THE COGO WORKPLACE WELLBEING SURVEY 2020

BACKGROUND

Understanding and supporting mental wellbeing in the workplace is increasingly a priority for many New Zealand and Australian employers. Auckland-based research agency Cogo designed the Workplace Wellbeing Survey 2020 to capture information from people in the workforce about their experience of health and wellbeing in their professional lives.

ABOUT COGO

Founded in 2014, Cogo has extensive experience in programme evaluation and insights research. Cogo works with a range of clients from the private, public and NGO sectors. Cogo has evaluated a wide range of projects aiming to bring about social change through improved mental and physical wellbeing, including multiple Ministry of Health-funded projects aimed at reducing New Zealand's obesity statistics through physical activity and improved nutrition, and the Health Promotion Agency's 'Play Your Best Card', a card-based game aimed at improving the mental health and wellbeing of young people.

Tania Domett (director) and Dr Jennie Coker (head of research) made up the Workplace Wellbeing Survey team, with over 18 and 13 years' experience respectively delivering applied research and evaluation.

SURVEY DESIGN

Cogo designed and built the Workplace Wellbeing Survey using advanced online survey software SurveyGizmo. The survey captured demographic data from respondents, as well as basic information about organisation size and sector, their role and their experience around stress and wellbeing in the workplace.

I engaged Cogo to gather information relating to workplace

burnout as part of the Workplace Wellbeing Survey for inclusion in *Beyond Burnout.* Collaboration and co-design is a critical part of Cogo's research process, and as such Cogo worked with me to build this section of the data-collection tool. The survey's questions were designed by drawing on my experience and secondary research in this area, on Maslach's Burnout Inventory, and also on Cogo's experience collecting information from employees in previous commercial work with clients. This survey section captured information that indicated whether respondents showed signs of exhaustion, isolation, lack of engagement, low professional efficacy, depersonalisation and cynicism.

The survey was distributed via a dedicated Facebook page (www.facebook.com/workplacewellbeingsurvey/), using paid advertising, and through Cogo's social media channels, including LinkedIn and Facebook. I also promoted the survey through my channels. Respondents qualified for the research if they were either currently in paid or volunteer work in New Zealand or

Australia, or had been in paid or volunteer work in the past six months. The survey was anonymous and respondents were incentivised with a prize-draw to win one of six $150 Visa gift cards.

SURVEY SAMPLE

The survey received 1525 complete responses from across all New Zealand regions and Australian states and territories. The sample includes 1195 responses from individuals in the New Zealand workforce and 330 from the Australian workforce. New Zealanders are therefore over-represented in the survey-data and meaningful comparison between countries was not possible.

The sample included 1169 responses from individuals identifying as female, 331 identifying as male, and 14 either identifying as Agender, Gender-fluid, Genderqueer or Non-binary, or answering Don't know/Questioning/Unsure for this question. Due to the over-representation of females in the sample, data was weighted to gender for analysis (i.e. all values presented in *Beyond Burnout* have been weighted to gender).

Survey questions relating to the burnout indicators discussed in *Beyond Burnout* were analysed as follows:

- Respondents were tagged as showing signs of exhaustion if they answered 'Every day' or 'A few times a week' to 'How often do you feel tired when you get up in the morning and have to face another day on the job?' and/or 'How often do you feel emotionally drained from your work?'
- Respondents were tagged as showing signs of isolation if they answered 'Every day' or 'A few times a week' to 'How often do you feel misunderstood or unappreciated by your co-workers?'
- Respondents were tagged as showing signs of depersonalisation if they answered 'Every day' or 'A few times a week' to 'How often do you feel that you are harder and less sympathetic with people at work than perhaps they deserve?' and/or 'How often are you easily

irritated by small problems or by your co-workers?'
- Respondents were tagged as showing signs of a lack of engagement if they answered 'Every day' or 'A few times a week' for 'How often do you think about leaving your current place of work?' and/or agreeing that '...recently you have become less enthusiastic about your work'.
- Respondents were tagged as showing signs of low professional efficacy if they answered 'Not very confident' or 'Not at all confident' to 'How confident are you that you are effective at getting things done at work?' and/or 'How confident are you that you can effectively solve problems that crop up in your work?'
- Finally, respondents showed one or both of the following signs of cynicism:
  —believing that they 'make a valuable contribution to the business or organisation' only a few times a month or less

—answering 'Every day' or 'A few times a week' to 'Work politics or bureaucracy get in the way of your ability to do a good job'.

For more information about Cogo please see www.cogo.co.nz or email tania@cogo.co.nz

APPENDIX B

THE STAGES OF BURNOUT

(USEFUL FOR THE 'RECOGNISE' STRATEGY)

Here are the different stages that indicate the progressive nature of burnout. It's not a purely linear progression, and can take hold subtly, over time. This list will give you some markers to help recognise it as it progresses, in yourself or others. These stages closely reflect my own experience of burnout and that of others who I have worked with.

STAGE 1

This stage is almost a 'precursor' to burnout. In particular with regard to the first bullet point below, an increase in energy may often be an initial response to overwork and trying to 'plough through', with increased effort to overcome the initial feelings of burnout.

- Lots of energy and enthusiasm. An almost hyper-focus or vigilance, over-conscientiousness
- Feeling overworked
- Feelings of uncertainty and self-doubt
- Doubts about coping with work

WARNING SIGNS

- Too busy to take holidays
- Reluctant to take days off
- Bringing work home regularly
- Spending too little time with partner/family or interests outside work which have historically been important
- Being frustrated with results
- Experiencing doubts about coping with work requirements, i.e. job demands exceeding job resources

STAGE 2

- Short-lived bouts of irritation or increased hostility towards co-workers, customers or other stakeholders
- Blaming others, scapegoating

- Increased tiredness and anxiety, trouble sleeping
- Detachment and distancing, especially from colleagues and/or customers/clients
- Increased feelings of stagnation, feeling as though 'I'm not getting anywhere'

WARNING SIGNS

- Making increasing numbers of complaints about the quality of others' work
- Unable to cope with the pressure of work commitments. Finding an ever-higher energy investment is required in order to execute all job tasks
- Working long hours
- Reduced ability to manage time efficiently or to concentrate
- Feeling overwhelmed by too many social or work commitments
- Sleep disturbances and susceptibility to headaches and other physical pain

STAGE 3

- General pervasive discontent with work/professional life
- Increasing anger/resentment
- Lowering of self-esteem and self-efficacy
- Growing feelings of guilt
- Lack of emotional commitment
- Apathy

WARNING SIGNS

- Lack of enjoyment of life outside of work as well as at work
- Extreme exhaustion
- Reduced commitment to work; just 'going through the motions'
- Reduced commitment to activities and engagement at home

STAGE 4

- Withdrawal and giving up
- Illness
- Feelings of failure
- Extreme personal distress, despair

WARNING SIGNS

- Increasing absenteeism or presenteeism, 'checking out'
- Avoiding colleagues. Aversion to oneself, to other people, to everything
- Reluctance to communicate
- Increasing isolation
- Physical ailments
- Alcohol or drug abuse
- Depression

APPENDIX C

STRESS IDENTIFICATION DIARY

(USEFUL FOR 'RECOGNISE' AND 'ORGANISE' STRATEGIES)

Identifying our sources of stress can be a useful exercise for anyone, anytime. But it becomes even more important in the context of preventing and treating burnout.

The purpose of this exercise is to identify those situations which cause you stress. We're more likely to feel stressed by workplace situations that are (or that we perceive to be) unexpected, unpredictable and out of our control. Remember, positive stress (eustress) is good for us and our performance. Not all stress is bad.

First, begin by reviewing and listing the workplace stressors you commonly experience. These may broadly be related to areas such as:

- conflict or working-relationship issues or workplace politics
- demands to do with the work itself
- a lack of clarity on expectations
- tight deadlines
- lack of resources, including time or equipment
- lack of knowledge or skill and a need for training and/or upskilling
- sense of unfairness
- lack of appreciation or recognition
- inadequate compensation
- conflict between your work and your values or integrity
- conflict between your personal and work responsibilities (e.g. difficulty in balancing the two).

List your most common *negative* workplace stressors, as in our example below. Be as specific as you can. Then, following the table provided, explore what *specifically* about these situations creates stress for you.

Finally, identify a specific time that you dealt effectively with these (or similar) stressors: what did you do, and what helped?

Workplace stressor (be specific)	Why this feels stressful to me	How have I dealt effectively with this stressor in the past?
• Conflict with a colleague	• My relationships at work are important to me. When there is conflict, it reduces productivity between us and I feel anxious.	• Talked it over with my manager and brainstormed ideas on how to address it. Looked at what I was doing that might be contributing. Had a talk with my colleague on how we could improve the main areas of conflict between us.

Now, identify those areas in your work life that are *positive* sources of eustress. Once again, be specific. Identify specifically what it is about these situations that creates that positive stress. Remember, eustress motivates us and focuses our energy. It is usually short term or finite in nature, it's something we perceive we can cope with, and it feels exciting and generally improves our performance.

Source of eustress	Why this is positive stress to me	How can I increase the opportunity to experience this in my work?
• Creating a new leadership workshop	• It pushes me outside my comfort zone, makes me learn something new, makes me grow and requires me to use creativity, which is a strength of mine.	• Develop strategy for increasing leadership workshops for my existing clients (business development and delivery) by end of March.

Once you've identified your negative stressors and reflected on how you have dealt successfully with these in the past, and have done the same with sources of eustress, spend the next two weeks keeping a stress diary. Notice when you experience that negative stress, and remind yourself how you have dealt successfully with it in the past. Try doing the same thing again in this situation. Write down how it felt to respond to the negative stress in this way. What was the outcome and what happened?

As well, during the same two weeks, focus in on the situations that provide you with eustress and notice when you

are in flow – that is, immersed in a feeling of energised focus, full involvement and enjoyment in the process of the activity. Notice what it feels like, and write this down in your stress diary.
- What are your insights from the above exercise?
- What are the common themes?

APPENDIX D

MONTHLY ONE-ON-ONES

(USEFUL FOR THE 'SOCIALISE' AND 'ORGANISE' STRATEGIES)

Of all the meetings we can have in our working diary, as a leader, your monthly or fortnightly one-on-one with each of your direct reports is one of the most important. They are a chance to check in with your team individually, without other distractions and influences—a chance to attend to the working relationship, rather than focusing only on the tasks that need to be completed. These sessions, then, are about working on the 'how' and the 'who', not just the 'what'.

Although your first response to the idea of scheduling (and sticking to) regular one-on-ones may be that you don't have time for another meeting, these get-togethers can save you countless hours of time and agony in the long run, as they tend to provide a vehicle for communication and the opportunity to nip problems in the bud before they become crises. They are also one of the most powerful strategies for reducing isolation, a key cause of burnout, provided they are done well.

If you think of the analogy of a ship which heads off from port on a significant journey to a distant but important destination (think the vision for the department or company), the captain of the ship (you) is constantly checking the ship is heading in the right direction, as well as checking that all the components of the ship are working. As a captain, you wouldn't set a course on the compass and check in to see if you're heading in the right direction only once or twice during the journey. Instead, you would check your bearings regularly to ensure that the winds and weather have not blown the ship off course. You would check the compass and equipment many times to ensure the ship was correctly headed for the desired destination. So it is with one-on-one meetings: they are a way to check your bearings with each member of your team.

It is easy in the day-to-day busyness, and with all the other demands on our time, to defer these meetings. But this is almost worse than not having them at all. Give them the same importance and value as you would a meeting with a chief customer—and reap the rewards as a result.

10 BENEFITS OF ONE-ON-ONES

1. To discover levels of motivation in each of your team members. How motivated are they? Is there anything that is going on in their private life that is having an impact on their work? What drives them to perform at their best? What, if anything, is hindering their motivation?
2. To address any performance issues before they become serious. Often, when we first notice an area for improvement with one of our direct reports, it may be minor. This is the time to talk about it, before it becomes a big

issue for them—and for you. One-on-ones are a great mechanism for feedback.
3. To give specific praise and highlight things your team member has done well in the period since the last meeting. This is such a great motivator and helps you to catch people doing the right things.
4. To ensure their Performance Development Plan (PDP) is a 'live' document and to ensure there are no surprises when you have an annual or six-monthly performance appraisal.
5. To receive feedback from them as to what you are doing that is supporting or hindering their progress, enabling the flow of communication to go both ways within an organisation.
6. To reinforce important messages about change or company direction and to garner feedback from them about various initiatives. (Do they support the change or not? What are their ideas? How is it affecting them?)

7. To brainstorm ideas and solutions for team problems or challenges. Remember, you don't have all the answers, and an issue that the team is having may be solved *by them.* This is especially the case if a team member is shy and less likely to pipe up in a team meeting.
8. To enable your team member to raise areas in their role they are struggling with and for you to coach them on them.
9. To strengthen the rapport and 'put money in the bank' for this vital working relationship.
10. To act as a litmus test for the mood of the team as a whole. If you meet with all of your team members individually in a month, you are bound to get a better read of how the team is going than if you did not.

Here's a sample agenda for one-on-ones:

Name:	
Month:	
Highlights/lowlights from previous month (direct report goes before leader):	
What did I learn from the above? What are we going to do moving forward as a result?	
Key priorities agreed from last month:	
Key achievements:	
Performance Development Plan/KPIs — how are we tracking? (List all KPIs or PDP goals and discuss how they're tracking and any support and action required.)	
How would you rate your wellbeing? Rate on a scale of 1–10, where 1 is awful and 10 is awesome.	
What is contributing to this score?	
Anything else top of mind? (Company initiatives/change/feedback to leader, etc.)	
Key priorities for next month:	

APPENDIX E

IDENTIFYING STRENGTHS AND ENCOURAGING PEOPLE TO WORK FROM THEM

(USEFUL FOR THE 'ORGANISE' AND 'SOCIALISE' STRATEGIES)

'Strengths are not activities you're good at, they're activities that strengthen you. A strength is an activity that before you're doing it you look forward to doing it; while you're doing it, time goes by quickly and you can concentrate; after you've done it, it seems to fulfil a need of yours.'
Marcus Buckingham, English author and business consultant, global expert on strengths

As we learnt in the chapter on the *Organise* strategy, when people work from their strengths it not only increases their engagement, it can also help protect them from burnout. Research has shown that it gives them a greater sense of control over their work and leads to higher engagement, productivity and performance.

The sweet-spot development model discussed here is a simple one I adapted from the Japanese concept of *ikigai* (which roughly means 'reason for being'). This is a practical model that you can use with your direct reports and your team as a whole to identify strengths and begin to work more from these strengths over time.

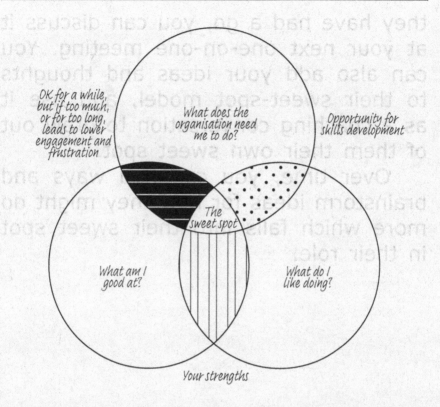

Here's how you can apply this model. First, try it out on yourself. Plot yourself on the model, filling out each circle and working out where they coincide to give you your own sweet spot.

Then, in your next one-on-one meeting with each of your direct reports, do the same exercise with them. Perhaps give them a heads-up and explain the model to them in one meeting, show them yours, then get them to go away and complete it. Once they have had a go, you can discuss it at your next one-on-one meeting. You can also add your ideas and thoughts to their sweet-spot model, and use it as a coaching conversation to draw out of them their own sweet spot.

Over time, you can find ways and brainstorm ideas for how they might do more which falls into their sweet spot in their role.

APPENDIX F
THE TIME MANAGEMENT MATRIX

(USEFUL FOR THE 'ORGANISE' STRATEGY)

This Time Management Matrix is a simple but effective tool for prioritising a to-do list based on the level of urgency and importance of each task. You may already know about this tool, by one of its various names.

Some people call it the 'Eisenhower Matrix'. Dwight Eisenhower was the Supreme Allied Commander in Europe during World War II, before becoming the president of Columbia University and then 34th President of the United States. He developed the basic system, so it's also sometimes called the Eisenhower Box or the Eisenhower Method.

Some people call it the Urgent-Important Matrix, and many call it 'the Covey Matrix', because Stephen

Covey described it in his book *The 7 Habits of Highly Effective People.* No matter what you call it, the matrix will help you increase your effectiveness and reduce your stress.

As a leader, it is a useful tool to teach your direct reports, to help them identify priorities, as well as being a useful time-management tool for yourself. It can help people to gain clarity on their most important tasks and therefore address both a lack of prioritisation and overwork. It helps people overcome the natural tendency to focus on urgent activities, so that we can keep enough clear time to focus on what's really important. This is a really useful way to move from 'firefighting' into a position of more control. And we know that a lack of control can be a cause of burnout.

Here are two of the basic premises of the model:
- 'Important' activities are those that have an outcome that leads to the achievement of your most important goals at work.
- Those activities which fall under the 'urgent' header are those which

tend to demand our immediate attention. They are often associated with the achievement of *someone else's* goals.

Not surprisingly, we often concentrate on the urgent activities, which demand our attention because the consequences of not dealing with them are immediate, rather than putting effort into what is actually important.

HOW TO USE THE TOOL

The matrix can be drawn as shown below, with the dimensions of importance and urgency.

	URGENT	NOT URGENT
IMPORTANT	① DO	② PLAN
NOT IMPORTANT	③ DELEGATE/ PUSH BACK	④ ELIMINATE

Follow the steps below to use the matrix to prioritise your activities:

1. The first step is to list all the activities and projects you currently have underway. Try to include everything that takes up your time at work, however unimportant. If you manage your time using a to-do list, you will already have a good idea of these.
2. Next, on a scale of 1 to 5, assign importance to each of the activities. Remember, this is a measure of how *important* the activity is in helping you meet your goals and objectives. Try not to worry about urgency at this stage.
3. Once you've assigned an importance value to each activity, evaluate its urgency. As you do this, plot each item on the matrix according to the values that you've given it.
4. Now study the matrix using the strategies described below to schedule your priorities.

STRATEGIES FOR DIFFERENT QUADRANTS OF THE MATRIX

Urgent and important

These are activities which need your immediate attention. There are two types of urgent and important activities: the first type are the activities that you could not foresee, and the second are things you've left to the last minute.

You can avoid last-minute activities by planning ahead and avoiding procrastination. Issues and crises, on the other hand, cannot always be foreseen or avoided. Here, the best approach is to leave some time in your schedule to handle unexpected issues and unplanned important activities. (If a major crisis arises, then you'll obviously need to reschedule other events.)

If you have a lot of urgent and important activities, identify which of these could have been foreseen, and think about how you could schedule similar activities ahead of time in the future, so that they don't become urgent.

Urgent and not important

Urgent but not important activities are things that stop you achieving your goals and prevent you from completing your work. Ask yourself whether these tasks can be rescheduled or whether you can delegate them.

Other people in your workplace are a common source of such interruptions. Sometimes it's appropriate to say 'no' to people politely, or to encourage them to solve the problem themselves. Alternatively, try scheduling time when you are available, so that people know that they can interrupt you at these times. (A good way of doing this is to schedule a regular meeting, so that all issues can be dealt with at the same time.) By doing this, you'll be able to concentrate on your important activities for longer periods of time.

Not urgent, but important

These are the activities that help you achieve your personal and professional goals, and complete important work. Make sure that you have plenty of time to do these things properly, so that they do not become urgent.

Once again, remember to leave enough time in your schedule to deal with unforeseen problems. This will maximise your chances of keeping on schedule, and help you avoid the stress of work becoming more urgent than necessary.

Not urgent and not important
These activities are just a distraction, and should be avoided if possible. Some can simply be ignored or cancelled. Others are activities that other people may want you to do, but they do not contribute to your own desired outcomes. Again, say 'no' politely, if you can.

If people see that you are clear about your objectives and boundaries, they will often not ask you to do 'not important' activities in the future.

*

The Time Management Matrix helps you look at your task list and quickly identify the activities you should focus on. By prioritising using the matrix, you can deal with truly urgent issues, while at the same time keep working towards important longer-term goals.

APPENDIX G

SOME USEFUL COACHING QUESTIONS FOR LEADERS

(USEFUL FOR ALL OF THE FOUR '-ISE' STRATEGIES—AND SKILLED LEADERSHIP IN GENERAL!)

The leadership skill of coaching is an immensely powerful one, to not only improve performance and engagement, but also to help prevent burnout. Coaching enhances a person's self-awareness. It also draws on a person's strengths and can help them to question or challenge self-defeating thoughts and beliefs. It helps an employee examine new perspectives and align their personal values with their professional responsibilities.

Here are some useful coaching questions that leaders can use with their direct reports to help them manage their work better, build social connection, and increase that person's

locus of control (how strongly they believe they have control over the situations and experiences that affect their work life).
- What do you want to achieve?
- How do you get in your own way? How do we get past it?
- If any actions were possible, what would they be?
- What will you do?
- How will you know?
- In a best-case scenario, what would X look like? What is the outcome you most want?
- What is the driver for you?
- If you can't achieve X, what will that be like?
- What results do you anticipate?
- What have you done so far?
- What has gone wrong in similar situations in the past?
- What are the possibilities?
- What are the potential obstacles?
- What options can you create?
- Where do we go from here?
- What would be your desired outcomes?
- What effect does that have (on you/others/the organisation)?

- What gets in the way of X happening?
- What is the worst-case scenario?
- Why is this important?
- What is the likelihood of this not working?
- Who needs to be involved?
- What really matters to you (and/or others) about this?
- What did you mean when you said...?
- What other angles have you thought about?
- Can you say a little more about that?
- What led up to that?
- What do you conclude from this?
- What strikes you about what we have just discussed?
- My understanding of what you said is ... Is that correct?
- How would you describe that?
- Can I just check my understanding...?

APPENDIX H

HOW TO IMPROVE YOUR EMOTIONAL INTELLIGENCE

(USEFUL FOR THE 'RECOGNISE', 'DESTIGMATISE' AND 'SOCIALISE' STRATEGIES)

Daniel Goleman, author of the book *Emotional Intelligence,* is viewed by many as the world-expert on this topic. Emotional intelligence (EQ) is our ability to manage our emotions. We often value IQ, but EQ is just as important, if not more important, for professional success. It focuses on awareness, self-regulation, motivation, empathy and social skills.

When it comes to burnout, studies have confirmed that there's a correlation between high levels of emotional intelligence and lower instances of burnout. There is a clear positive relationship between EQ and burnout. In other words, the higher the emotional intelligence of a particular individual, the less likely they are to experience burnout. What's more, people who are emotionally intelligent make better leaders.

FIVE WAYS YOU CAN IMPROVE YOUR EMOTIONAL INTELLIGENCE

1. Build your self-awareness. The Ancient Greeks had it nailed when they said 'Know thyself'. Understand *why* you have the view of the world that you do and what influences have shaped this view. Know your own backstory, where you have come from, where you get tripped up, your own triggers and, conversely, what lights you up. You can build your self-awareness by doing things like participating in a 360-degree feedback exercise, or by taking a free online strengths assessment like the VIA Character Strengths survey, Clifton Strengths (formerly Clifton Strengths Finder) or the

Red Bull 'Wingfinder' personality assessment. If you're a leader, regularly ask your direct reports what they want you to stop doing, keep doing, start doing and do more of, in order for you to lead them better. And don't let them stop until they have at least two things under the first point! Ask your direct manager and peers what they think your strengths, weaknesses and under-utilised skills are.

2. Reflect. Make time for reflection, as well as action. Mindfulness, journalling and exercising in solitude are all ways to help you tune in to yourself more effectively.

3. Practise empathy. Put yourself in the other person's shoes. This seems obvious, but consciously focusing on doing this when another person begins to share their perspective helps to develop empathy. Focus on the feelings and situations that you have experienced in the past that are similar. This will deepen your

emotional insight into the other person's perspective.
4. Listen—deeply and actively. Listen with all your senses, not just to the words that are being spoken by another person. Reserve judgement for as long as you can. Don't interrupt. Stop that internal story in your head and just tune in to what the other person is saying. Paraphrase to check your assumptions.
5. Be curious. Cultivate curiosity about people, especially those who are very different from you (even your 'enemies' or competitors). Being non-judgementally inquisitive about the world in which we live is something children do naturally. Take a leaf out of their book and seek to understand people more deeply.

APPENDIX I

DELEGATION MODEL

(USEFUL FOR THE 'ORGANISE' STRATEGY)

Delegation is a useful strategy to combat overwork and organise workflow more effectively. This is especially useful if you are a leader. Here is a simple model for how to delegate effectively.

STEP ONE: WHAT WILL I DELEGATE? AND TO WHOM?

Delegate smartly—for development and team effectiveness. This is not about dumping stuff you hate doing. Work out what areas you need to keep (strategy, for example) and what areas you could delegate (i.e. a task which is repetitive and not the best use of your time). Make a list:

- These are the areas I need to keep:

- These are some tasks that I could currently delegate:

Involve your team members in the decision on what to delegate to them. This is also a great way to incorporate focus from what you have agreed are their areas for development. Ask each one of them:
- Where do you need and want to develop further?
- What areas of my job could you help me with?
- In looking at specific tasks I could delegate, where do you feel more confident? Where are you less confident?

STEP TWO: START WITH A CLEAR PICTURE OF WHAT SUCCESS IS

One of the biggest problems with delegation starts right at the beginning, when you're delivering the work to the person. Make sure you are clear in giving instructions and the context of the task. Get them to feed back to you what the ideal outcome looks like.

Ensure clarity on the end game, expectations and timeframes.

Good questions can include:
- What will success look like? How will we know when we have achieved our goal?
- What do you want to learn here?
- How will it feel? What will we both be seeing and feeling if this is successful?
- What aspects of this task do you feel *most* confident about?
- What aspects of this task do you feel *least* confident about?
- What support do you need from me along the way?
- Who are the key stakeholders, and what do they need for this to be successful?

STEP THREE: IDENTIFY THE MOST USEFUL PROCESS, AND CHECKPOINTS, TO ENSURE SUCCESS

One of the most common missteps when delegating is to hand over the task without giving due thought to

safety nets, support and decision-making processes. Therefore, before you set your person off on their merry way, it's worth having a conversation on the following topics:
- What checkpoints will we put in place along the way to ensure we are both comfortable with progress?
- On what aspects will you consult with me before making decisions? Here are areas which I see as critical points...
- What feedback loops do we need to put in place? How often, or at what points, will you check in with me on this task?

Remember: have realistic expectations regarding the time it will take at first and the person's skill level. Think about the first time you did this task; chances are, you weren't as skilled and fast as you are now. Build in achievable timeframes and set realistic expectations for learners.

STEP FOUR: GET OUT OF THE WAY

A common mistake leaders make when delegating is to go through the motions of delegation and then do what I call 'the hover'. If the steps above have been done well and thoroughly, you can then get out of their way.

STEP FIVE: REVIEW

After the work has been completed, ensure you both sit down together and review what worked, what didn't, and what you both learned. This review is the perfect opportunity for a coaching session. This is perhaps the most critical step in successful delegation, yet it is often overlooked.

- Useful questions for discussion at this point include the following: 'Let's talk about what went well...' Get them to go first in describing what went well. Follow it up with '...and what did you learn from that?'
- 'What didn't go so well? What aspects of the project or task did

you find difficult or stumble on?' Once again, get them to go first and then offer your observations.
- 'What did you learn?' ... 'and what else?'
- 'What did I do that was helpful during the process? What could I do next time to improve my support and help you learn more? Anything you want me to stop doing next time?'

You might be thinking, 'But what if I'm not delegating because my team is already overworked?' This is generally a sign of a lack of prioritisation, given the current resources. Leaders in organisations are often being asked to 'do more with less', so if increasing your people resources is not an option in the current environment, take a closer look at Greg McKeown's book *Essentialism*. It may mean you and your team have too many priorities or are trying to do too much with the current resources and time available. You may need to negotiate with *your* direct manager around which are the key priorities for a specified period of time, and what you and your team need to stop doing, or delay, given current resources.

APPENDIX J

A PRACTICAL EXERCISE FOR BUILDING A COLLECTIVE VISION AND TRUST WITH YOUR TEAM

(USEFUL FOR THE 'SOCIALISE' AND 'ORGANISE' STRATEGIES)

Building a high-performing, cohesive team is one of your most imperative responsibilities as a leader. It also goes some way to safeguarding you and your team from burnout.

Sounds obvious, huh? But too often it's something we leave to chance, instead of being purposeful and committed to proactively creating. Building a high-performing and cohesive team requires intentional practice—and, perhaps more importantly, persistence. It takes time. I would also add in this case, '...and only if you're purposeful and committed to it!'

So what makes a high-performing, trust-filled and cohesive team? A successful team maximises the talents of its individual members, but the true power of teamwork comes from the group's cohesion and combined energies focused on a common goal.

Your first priority is to build trust within your team—and for them with you. If you don't have trust within your team, you're in for a very bumpy ride. It also means collectively getting clear on what success looks like—'true north', as it were.

But where to start? Below is a simple, practical exercise (which is featured in my blended leadership programme for emerging leaders, The Leader's Map), which gets you started on that road to creating a high-performing, cohesive team. It helps you and your team collectively build a picture of success. And it helps you answer important questions like:

- What specifically does it look like if we are a high-performing team? (Remember, this will be different for different teams.)

- What will we be seeing and feeling if we achieve this picture of success?
- How will we *know* we have achieved this picture of success? How will we measure our progress towards this picture? What will our key stakeholders be saying about us?
- What might be the potential roadblocks facing us as a team when it comes to achieving this picture of success? And what are some ideas for overcoming these roadblocks?
- What will be the first, actionable steps we'll take to move towards this picture of success? (Here you might think about things like meetings, operating rhythms, agreed behaviours, decision-making approaches, etc.)

In my experience of facilitating, a positive by-product of these sorts of sessions is that they help to build trust. They also help a team to answer the questions 'What is our purpose and why are we even here?' and 'What do we want?' Pretty important questions, in my opinion!

HOW TO RUN THIS SESSION WITH YOUR TEAM

1. Set aside two hours with your team. Off-site and private is ideal in terms of location, but an uninterrupted two hours, where people have their phones switched off and are fully present, is the most important thing. Ensure you have giant flipcharts, coloured markers, Post-its and pens at the ready.
2. Let your team members know in advance the purpose of the session and what's in it for them.
3. Give them some 'pre-work'. Ask them to think and jot down their answers to the bullet-pointed questions on the previous page. Let them know that there are no right or wrong answers—any idea is a good idea at this stage. However, do encourage them to be as specific as possible. For example, 'we have high trust' is a start, but it's too broad. 'We openly share our challenges and

ask each other for help when we need it' is a signpost of trust that is more specific.
4. Tell them you will be working with their pre-work ideas in the session. Asking them to think of answers ahead of time will help them to focus on what you'll cover in the session and gives them some hints on what to expect. It's especially useful for introverts, who like to think about their answers in advance rather than contributing on the fly, and it encourages individual ideas and contribution.
5. Start your session by reiterating the purpose (as above) and asking what each person wants to get out of the session, in a structured round. Note these down on a flipchart. Then, collectively set up the ground rules for the session. Examples of ground rules might be: practise active listening to each other; be open to ideas; no idea is a bad idea at first; one person speaking at a time.

6. Next, divide into small groups (of three or four people) and get each group to discuss, share and write on their respective flipcharts the answers to the following questions (give them approximately 30 minutes to do this):

—**Success looks like ...** What specifically does it look like if we are a high-performing team? What will we be seeing and feeling if we achieve this picture of success? What will our key stakeholders be saying about us?

—**How will we *know*...?** How will we know we have achieved this picture of success? How will we measure our progress towards this picture?

—**Potential roadblocks to success ...** What might be the potential roadblocks facing us as a team when it comes to achieving this picture of success? How might we get in our own way?

—**How we will achieve this? (specific actions)** What will be the first, actionable steps we will take to move towards this picture of success? Think meetings, operating rhythms, agreed behaviours, decision-making approaches.

7. After 30 minutes or so of discussion and idea generation, get each group to report their top three ideas from each section back to the full team. Capture these on a separate flipchart. Discuss the common themes and differences among the team.
8. As a team, decide on the clear answers to each bullet point above. Use voting or discussion to do this.
9. Agree on who is going to do what next as a result of your insights. In other words, relook at the fourth bullet—the next steps and specific actions—and assign responsibilities and timeframes as a result of the session. Assign tasks of recording and follow-up, and make sure you're all on the same page about what decisions have been made.
10. Book another review session for two months' time to assess your

progress. Remember, this is just the start!

An important hint for you as leader: Aim to act primarily as facilitator, so go last with your ideas—and don't dominate the conversation. Ask powerful coaching questions to help people think and draw out their ideas. The purpose of this exercise is to harness the ideas of the team and get them excited and on board, working towards the ideal state.

APPENDIX K

THE WHEEL OF LIFE

(USEFUL FOR THE 'RECOGNISE' AND 'ORGANISE' STRATEGIES)

In her book *A Slight Detour,* author and executive coach Jayne Chater has a simple but powerful tool to assess the balance of your life. It helps you visualise all the important areas of your life at once, to better understand which areas of your life are flourishing and which ones need the most work. She has graciously let me use her Wheel of Life exercise here.

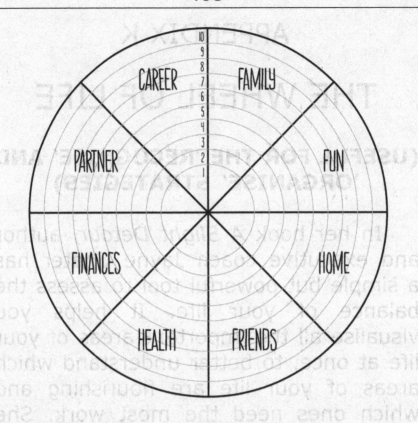

EXERCISE: THE WHEEL OF LIFE

This exercise is geared towards helping you assess the different areas of your life holistically.

First, identify eight key areas of your life, by brainstorming all the things that are important to you. From there, you'll need to rank them so you can come up with a list of the eight that are the most important. Each person's will

differ, but some of the areas that people often identify or choose include:
- Career/work
- Personal development and growth
- Friends
- Family
- Partner or significant other
- Finances
- Spiritual life
- Your physical environment (where you live and, perhaps, *how* you are living)
- Fun and recreation
- Health and vitality
- Emotional wellbeing
- Social life

Once you've got your list of eight, label each of the segments on the 'wheel' as being representative of one of your eight areas. Envisage that the centre point of your wheel represents 0 and the outer edge of each 'spoke' represents 10.

Next, score each aspect of your life that you've identified—each segment—out of 10, where 1 means that you're really unsatisfied with where you're at regarding that area currently, and 10 means you are totally satisfied.

If you think of each spoke of the wheel as a continuum, you can make a mark in different places along each line to mark your score. Joining these marks together then provides you with a view of how balanced (or wonky!) your life is at that point in time.

APPLYING IT FURTHER, PRACTICALLY

The Wheel of Life exercise is a great way to take a snapshot of your life and assess your priorities, which are the foundation of your roadmap for where you put time and energy into on an ongoing basis. However, it's one thing to know where you're at and another to act to improve it. See whether you can note down one or two things that could be changed for you to increase your score for each of the segments (unless you've got one that you've given a 10—in which case, well done!)

While you could get caught up in trying to change all of these things at once, that's likely to feel overwhelming. Instead, it's usually more realistic to pick one or two areas and focus on making the changes required to those aspects.

You might decide that the lowest three scores are the ones to work on first. Or it might be that you're OK with 'parking' one of them for now, knowing that you'll return to it more proactively later when time allows.

Think about who you might need to share your planned actions with: your partner? Family? Boss? Colleagues? Friends? Once you've made your action list, set another date with yourself to revisit this exercise. Because it takes a snapshot of your current situation, it pays to do it periodically. Some opt for monthly or quarterly, while others do it twice a year. I believe the ideal frequency is what feels right and useful for you—and that might be reflective of how much change you have going on at any one point (with more changes, you might feel more inclined to check in with where you're at more often).

Top tip: Always make sure that health (or wellbeing) is one of your top priorities. If you don't have your health, everything else that you are trying to juggle will crumble around you.

WHAT THIS EXERCISE MEANS FOR YOUR WORK LIFE

There's no doubt that work is a big component of our lives and, often, our identities. For some of us, it also takes up the majority of our energy. However, there are other things that are important to us, whether that be family, travel, being financially independent, our health, friendships, community or services, spirituality, sport ... the list goes on.

APPENDIX L

FURTHER RESOURCES

BOOKS I RECOMMEND

Elbin, Scott. *Overworked and Overwhelmed: The Mindfulness Alternative.* Wiley, 2014.

Evans, Dr Ceri. *Perform Under Pressure.* HarperCollins, 2019.

Lencioni, Patrick. *The Five Dysfunctions of a Team: A Leadership Fable,* Jossey-Bass, 2002.

Maslach, Christina and Michael P. Leiter. *The Truth About Burnout: How Organizations Cause Personal Stress and What to Do About It.* Jossey-Bass, 2000.

McKeown, Greg. *Essentialism: The Disciplined Pursuit of Less.* Currency, 2014.

Pang, Alex Soojung-Kim. *Rest: Why You Get More Done When You Work Less.* Basic Books, 2016.

Stallard, Michael L., et al. *Fired Up or Burned Out: How to Reignite Your Team's Passion, Creativity, and Productivity.* HarperCollins Leadership, 2009.

The Drexler Sibbet Team Performance Model. This is not a book, but it is a useful team performance model.

Zolli, Andrew and Ann Marie Healy. *Resilience: Why Things Bounce Back.* Free Press, 2012.

TOOLS FOR MEASURING BURNOUT IN THE WORKPLACE

The following surveys are designed to measure burnout in the workplace:
- *The Maslach Burnout Inventory—Human Services Survey for Medical Personnel* (MBI-HSS MP)

is a 22-item survey that covers three areas: Emotional Exhaustion (EE), Depersonalisation (DP) and low sense of Personal Accomplishment (PA). Each subscale includes multiple questions, with frequency-rating choices of Never, A few times a year or less, Once a month or less, A few times a month, Once a week, A few times a week, or Every day.

- *The Oldenburg Burnout Inventory*—a 16-item survey with positively and negatively framed items that cover two areas: exhaustion (physical, cognitive and affective aspects) and disengagement from work (negative attitudes towards work objects, work content, or work in general). There are multiple questions for each of these subscales and responses are in the form of a four-point Likert scale from Strongly agree (1) to Strongly disagree (4).

Finally, two of the best resources I've come across in New Zealand when it comes to addressing workplace mental wellbeing are:

- The website run by the Mental Health Foundation, www.mentalhealth.org.nz. It's full of practical ideas, resources and tips for organisations, leaders and individuals, so check it out!
- The Mentemia App. Co-founded by Sir John Kirwan and Adam Clark, Mentemia is packed with evidence-based ideas and tools to help you learn how to be well and stay well. It's for organisations and individuals alike. Check it out at www.mentemia.com.

REFERENCES

INTRODUCTION

'A survey by Blind...'

https://www.teamblind.com/blog/index.php/2020/05/05/burnout-has-risen-by-12-due-to-covid-19/

1. THE COST OF BURNOUT

'The burnout of employees is a symptom...'

https://blog.mcquaig.com/hidden-cost-of-burnout

'According to some researchers...'

Kaschka, W.P., Korczak, D., and Broich, K. (2011). Burnout: A fashionable diagnosis. *Deutsches Ärzteblatt Int. 108:*781. doi: 10.3238/arztebl.2011.0781

'their burnout rate is ... more than 50 per cent...'

Patti, M.G., Schlottmann, F., and Sarr, M.G. (2018). The problem of burnout among surgeons. *JAMA Surgery, 153* (5), 403–404. doi: 10.1001/jamasurg.2018.0047

'Early indications from research do show that Covid-19...'

https://www.nzdoctor.co.nz/article/undoctored/covid-19-mental-health-concerns-lead-kiwi-families-seek-professional-help-study

'An economic analysis commissioned by ... Korn Ferry...'

https://www.kornferry.com/insights/articles/the-trillion-dollar-difference

'O.C. Tanner 2020 Global Culture Report'

https://www.octanner.com/content/dam/oc-tanner/documents/white-papers/2019/INT-GCR2020-12.pdf

'A US survey conducted by Kronos Incorporated and Future Workplace...'

'American Psychological Association (APA) in their study "Paying with Our Health"...'

https://www.apa.org/news/press/releases/stress/2014/stress-report.pdf

'burnout will become a global pandemic in ten years...'

https://www.weforum.org/agenda/2016/10/workplace-burnout-can-you-do-anything-about-it

https://www.businesswire.com/news/home/20170109005377/en/Employee-Burnout-Crisis-Study-Reveals-Big-Workplace

2. MYTHS OF BURNOUT

'For the great enemy of truth...'

https://www.americanrhetoric.com/speeches/jfkyalecommencement.htm

'As social psychologist Christina Maslach...'

https://hbrascend.org/topics/burnout-is-about-your-workplace-not-your-people/

'A five-year study in the UK...'

https://www.personneltoday.com/pr/2017/05/corporate-burnout-affecting-the-mental-health-of-20-percent-of-top-performers-in-uk-businesses/

'An article in the *Harvard Business Review*...'

https://hbr.org/2018/06/how-are-you-protecting-your-high-performers-from-burnout

'an article for Silicon Republic...'

https://www.siliconrepublic.com/advice/beware-burnout-work-high-performers

'a Yale research study...'

https://www.emerald.com/insight/content/doi/10.1108/CDI-12-2016-0215/full/html

'2018 American Psychological Association survey...'

http://www.apaexcellence.org/assets/general/2018-work-and-wellbeing-survey-results.pdf

'1997 study of 76 clerical employees in Israel...'

https://qz.com/work/1660743/going-on-vacation-wont-cure-job-burnout/

'The National Center for Biotechnology Information...'

https://pubmed.ncbi.nlm.nih.gov/27158959/

'In one study of 2772 healthcare workers...'

https://academic.oup.com/occmed/article/64/4/279/1464114

3. WHAT IS BURNOUT?

'Pressure is a positive in a business environment...'

https://www.bbc.com/news/magazine-15573121

'Once we recognise burnout for the pandemic it is...'

https://www.weforum.org/agenda/2019/10/burnout-mental-health-pandemic/

'a massive research study at the University of Wisconsin...'

https://www.ncbi.nlm.nih.gov/pmc/articles/PMC3374921/

'a meta-analysis study by Panagiota Koutsimani...'

https://www.frontiersin.org/articles/10.3389/fpsyg.2019.00284/ full

'Both burnout and depression have been associated with...'

https://academicworks.cuny.edu/cgi/viewcontent.cgi?article=1328&context=cc_pubs

'The prevailing belief...'

https://www.psychologytoday.com/nz/blog/pressure-proof/201510/5-myths-about-burnout-and-the-truth-we-need-understand

4. WHO IS MOST AT RISK OF BURNOUT?

'No matter what job you do...'

https://qz.com/work/1635848/how-to-tell-if-youre-suffering-from-burnout-at-work/

'A 2010 meta study of over 400 studies...'

https://www.researchgate.net/publication/229389297_Gender_differences_in_burnout_A_meta-analysis

'2018 Grant Thornton International Women in Business Annual Report...'

https://www.grantthornton.co.nz/globalassets/1.-member-firms/new-zealand/pdfs/grant-thornton-women-in-business-2018.pdf

'For instance, women are more likely...'

https://www.sciencedirect.com/science/article/abs/pii/S0001879110000771

'Men and women report different reactions...'

https://www.apa.org/news/press/releases/stress/2010/gender-stress

'Research by Gabriella Gustafsson at Umea University...'

Gustafsson, G., Persson. B., Eriksson, Sture., Norberg, A. and Strandberg, G. (2009). Personality Traits among Burnt out and Non-Burnt out Health-Care Personnel at the Same Workplaces: A Pilot Study. *International Journal of Mental Health Nursing 18* (5): 336–48.

Doi: 10.1111/j.1447-0349.2009.00623.x

'Recent research looking at burnout in surgeons...'

Patti, M.G., Schlottmann, F., and Sarr, M.G. (2018). The problem of burnout among surgeons. *JAMA Surgery, 153* (5), 403–404. doi: 10.1001/jamasurg.2018.0047

'another 2013 study of senior managers and C-suite executives...'

https://arielle.com.au/c-suite-burnout-survey-summary/

'A survey by RHR International...'

https://hbr.org/2012/02/its-time-to-acknowledge-ceo-lo

5. WHAT CAUSES BURNOUT?

'Self Determination Theory (SDT)'

Legault, L. (2017) Self-Determination Theory. In: Zeigler-Hill V., Shackelford T. (Eds) Encyclopedia of Personality and Individual Differences. Springer, Cham. doi: 10.1007/978-3-319-28099-8_1162-1

'the US is the most overworked developed nation...'

https://20somethingfinance.com/american-hours-workedproductivity-vacation/

'OECD Better Life Index'

http://www.oecdbetterlifeindex.org/countries/new-zealand/

'a study published in 2014 by John Pencavel of Stanford University'

http://ftp.iza.org/dp8129.pdf

'Another study showed that "increasing a team's hours"...'

https://www.inc.com/jessica-stillman/why-working-more-than-40-hours-a-week-is-useless.html 'the story of diminishing returns...'

https://hbr.org/2015/08/the-research-is-clear-long-hours-backfire-for-people-and-for-companies

'Stress-related health problems make up between 75 and 90 per cent of hospital visits'

https://www.webmd.com/balance/stress-management/effects-of-stress-on-your-body#:~:text=Seventy%2Dfive%20percent%20to%2090,arthritis%2C%20depression%2C%20and%20 anxiety

'according to another study, managers couldn't tell the difference...'

https://pubsonline.informs.org/doi/abs/10.1287/orsc.2015.0975

'A study co-authored by Liuba Belkin...'

Belkin, L., Becker, W. and Conroy, S. (2020). The invisible leash: The impact of organizational expectations for email monitoring after-hours on employee resources, well-being, and turnover intentions. *Group & Organization Management.* doi: 10.1177/1059601120933143.

'In one study researchers gave the members of one group...'

Langer, E.J. (1989). Mindful aging. In *Mindfulness* (pp.82–85). Addison Wesley.

'Cigna study...'

https://www.cigna.com/static/www-cigna-com/docs/about-us/newsroom/studies-and-reports/combatting-loneliness/cigna-2020-loneliness-report.pdf

'2018 Gallup survey...'

https://www.gallup.com/workplace/237059/employee-burnout-part-main-causes.aspx#:~:text=Employees%20who%20strongly%20agree%20that,feeling%20uniformed%2C%20 alone%20and%20dismissive

'A longitudinal study by Jan Fekke Ybema...'

https://www.eurofound.europa.eu/publications/article/2008/lack-of-fairness-and-reward-for-efforts-can-lead-to-burnout-and-poor-job-satisfaction

'Employees who feel they're treated unfairly at work...'

https://www.gallup.com/workplace/237059/employee-burnout-part-main-causes.aspx

'As Michael Leiter and Christina Maslach put it...'

Leiter, M.P., & Maslach, C. (2004). Areas of worklife: A structured approach to organizational predictors of job burnout. In P. Perrewé & D.C. Ganster (Eds.), *Research in occupational stress and well being: Vol.3. Emotional and physiological processes and positive intervention strategies* (pp.91–134). JAI Press/Elsevier.

6. WHAT WE CAN DO TO ADDRESS BURNOUT

'Organisations that prioritise employee engagement...'

https://www.ipsos.com/ipsos-mori/en-uk/ftse-100-public-reporting-employee-wellness-engagement

'Organisations without systems to support the wellbeing of their employees...'

https://www.apa.org/news/press/releases/stress/2014/stress-report.pdf

'A number of studies have shown a direct link...' https://www.sciencedirect.com/science/article/abs/pii/S0025619615000713

'Higher levels of leadership support...'

Halbesleben, J.R.B. (2006). Sources of social support and burnout: A meta-analytic test of the conservation of resources model. *Journal of Applied Psychology, 91* (5), 1134–1145.

7. RECOGNISE

'Not knowing why, is, itself...'

Nagoski, E and Nagoski, A. Burnout: The Secret to Unlocking the Stress Cycle. Ballantine Books. 2020.

'research has shown that women...'

https://www.sciencedirect.com/science/article/abs/pii/S0001879110000771

8. DESTIGMATISE

'Shame never drives positive behaviour.'

https://www.marieforleo.com/2017/09/brene-brown/

'The World Health Organization (WHO) considers stigma to be one of the greatest barriers...'

Orel, E.T. (2007). Stigmatization in the long-term treatment of psychotic disorders. *Neuro-Endocrinology Letters, 28*, 35–45.

'three biggest barriers to speaking out'

Williford, M.L., et al. (2018). Multiple-institution comparison of resident and faculty perceptions of burnout and depression during surgical training. *JAMA Surgery, 153* (8), 705–711. doi: 10.1001/jamasurg.2018.0974

'burnout was stigmatised at only a slightly lower level than depression...'

Bianchi, R., Verkuilen, J., Brisson, R., Schonfeld, I.S., & Laurent, E. (2016). Burnout and depression: label-related stigma, help-seeking, and syndrome overlap. *Psychiatry Research, 245*, 91–98. doi: 10.1016/j.psychres.2016.08.025

'other findings indicate that burnout may not be less stigmatised than depression...'

Mendel, R., Kissling, W., Reichhart, T., Buhner, M., & Hamann, J. (2015). Managers' reactions towards employees' disclosure of psychiatric or somatic diagnoses. *Epidemiology and Psychiatric Science, 24,* 146–149. doi: 10.1017/s2045796013000711

'Because companies are not doing enough...'

https://hbr.org/2019/10/research-people-want-their-employers-to-talk-about-mental-health

'Burnout can be contagious...'

https://www.ncbi.nlm.nih.gov/pmc/articles/PMC7080824/

'experts tell us that one in four adults will struggle with a mental health issue...'

https://www.nami.org/mhstats

'a BBC article, "Stress: Is it surprising bosses are stricken?"...'

https://www.bbc.com/news/magazine-15573121

'The latest ground-breaking research published in *Scientific American*...'

https://blogs.scientificamerican.com/observations/mental-illness-is-far-more-common-than-we-knew/?

'In the Deloitte survey...'

https://www2.deloitte.com/us/en/pages/about-deloitte/articles/burnout-survey.html

9. SOCIALISE

'define connection as the energy...'

Brown, B. The Gifts of Imperfection. Hazelden Publishing. 2010.

'a meta study of over 148 studies...'

https://journals.plos.org/plosmedicine/article?id=10.1371/journal.pmed.1000316

'2018 Australian Loneliness Report...'

https://psychweek.org.au/2018-archive/loneliness-study/

'40 per cent of those under 25 globally are lonely...'

https://finance.yahoo.com/news/yales-famous-happiness-professor-dismantled-worlds-loneliness-epidemic-one-talk-123812658.html

'The General Social Survey in the US...'

https://time.com/3748090/friends-social-health/

'2016 New Zealand General Social Survey...'

https://treasury.govt.nz/publications/research-and-commentary/rangitaki-blog/new-wellbeing-analysis-mental-health-and-loneliness

'A recent study by Australian HR think tank Reventure of just over 1000 employees...'

http://www.afuturethatworks.org.au/media-stories/2019/7/8/40-of-australians-feel-lonely-at-work

'In a *Fast Company* article...'

https://www.fastcompany.com/3036935/why-you-need-to-actually-talk-to-your-coworkers-face-to-face

'EY Belonging Barometer...'

https://www.ey.com/en_us/diversity-inclusiveness/ey-belonging-barometer-workplace-study

'Burnout at Work Isn't Just About Exhaustion. It's Also About Loneliness.'

https://hbr.org/2017/06/burnout-at-work-isnt-just-about-exhaustion-its-also-about-loneliness

'one meta study looking at the impact of restructuring on employee wellbeing...'

de Jong, T., Wiezer, N., de Weerd, M., Nielsen, K., Mattila-Holappa, P. &

Mockałło, Z. (2015). The impact of restructuring on employee well-being: A systematic review of longitudinal studies. *Work and Stress* (in press). doi: 10.1080/02678373.2015.1136710

'Research by Andrew K. Przybylski and Netta Weinstein...'

https://www.scientificamerican.com/article/how-your-cell-phone-hurts-your-relationships/

'Melissa Lamson, an expert on leading virtual teams...'

https://www.inc.com/melissa-lamson/3-strategies-to-successfully-lead-virtual-teams.html

'bullying is associated with an increase in burnout...'

https://pubmed.ncbi.nlm.nih.gov/25082131/#:~:text=Results%3A%20Bullying%20is%20positively%20associated,strong%20negative%20toll%20on%20nurses.

'A global ICF study...'

https://instituteofcoaching.org/coaching-overview/coaching-benefits

'A study by the University of Columbia...'

https://www.telegraph.co.uk/education-and-careers/0/rising-epidemic-workplace-loneliness-have-no-office-friends/

10. ORGANISE

'2008 Harvard Business School survey of 1000 professionals...'

https://hbr.org/2009/10/making-time-off-predictable-and-required

'thought-provoking study of professional soccer goalies...'

Bar-Eli, M., Azar, O.H,. Ritov, I, Keidar-Levin, Y, Schein, G,. 'Action bias among elite soccer goalkeepers: The case of penalty kicks' https://mpra.ub.uni-muenchen.de/4477/1/MPRA_paper

'As James Surowiecki noted in his *New Yorker* article...'

https://www.newyorker.com/magazine/2014/01/27/the-cult-of-overwork

'As authors Eric M. Anicich and Jacob B. Hirsh point out...'

https://hbr.org/2017/03/why-being-a-middle-manager-is-so-exhausting

'McKinsey Global research, surveying a large set of global executives...'

https://www.mckinsey.com/business-functions/organization/our-insights/getting-organizational-redesign-right

'a Harvard research study...'

https://hbr.org/2017/04/if-you-think-downsizing-might-save-your-company-think-again

'research conducted by O.C. Tanner for their 2020 Global Culture Report...'

https://www.octanner.com/content/dam/oc-tanner/documents/white-papers/2019/INT-GCR2020-12.pdf

'Research has shown us that the more people feel involved in the creation of something...'

https://www.octanner.com/insights/white-papers/4-ways-to-prevent-employee-burnout.html

'monthly one-on-ones decrease burnout by 39 per cent...'

https://www.octanner.com/insights/white-papers/4-ways-to-prevent-employee-burnout.html

11. SO YOU THINK YOU MIGHT HAVE BURNOUT – NOW WHAT?

'too much high-intensity exercise...'

https://www.drlibby.com/health-wellbeing/is-there-such-a-thing-as-too-much-exercise/

'mindfulness programmes have been shown to reduce burnout...'

https://pubmed.ncbi.nlm.nih.gov/22849035/

APPENDIX H

'Studies have confirmed that there's a correlation between high levels of emotional intelligence and lower instances of burnout...'

https://www.hsj.gr/medicine/the-relationship-between-burnout-syndrome-and-emotional-intelligence-in-healthcare-professionals.php?aid=11303

ACKNOWLEDGEMENTS

I don't think this book would have been written had it not been for a man I came across on Twitter six years ago, who seemed to regularly pop up on my feed with pearls of wisdom on writing and leadership. He lives all the way across the world in America, and his name is Wally Bock. He has been a book coach extraordinaire, an expert book project-manager and a wealth of knowledge on leadership. These days, I feel privileged to call him a friend, too. And I still haven't met him face to face! Wally, thank you for your insight, patience and phenomenal skill on all things leadership, book writing and life in general.

My deepest gratitude also goes to Christina Wedgwood from Intelligent Ink. Your editing skills are beyond measure and your turnaround time leaves me breathless. Like Wally, you've been pivotal to this book being written. You are also an amazing human being, just BTW FYI.

To my publisher, Margaret Sinclair at Penguin Random House. When I first met you in that café on the North Shore, I knew it was a long shot that you'd take on a first-time nonfiction Kiwi author who wanted to write a book on burnout. But take a chance you did. I have been so fortunate for your and your team's guidance and skill, including Rachel Eadie, Sarah Ell, Grace Thomas, Lauren McKay, Becky Innes and Bex Argar. I have particularly valued all of your collaborative and supportive approaches throughout this process. I was a fan of Penguin Random House New Zealand before; I'm a raving one now.

To those people who allowed us to interview them and hear their stories for this book: thank you so very much for sharing your experience so that others may learn and feel less alone.

Tania Domett and Jennie Coker from Cogo Research—you were as excited about this project as I was. And that's saying something! The research you did in the Cogo Workplace Wellbeing Survey 2020, which we have used in this book, has been phenomenal. It has added robustness, as well as a uniquely Antipodean lens and depth to this book. Thank you also to Rachel Sinclair for giving up your weekend to read an early version of the draft!

To John Kirwan, thank you for writing the foreword for this book. I am both honoured and grateful. And I am in awe of the incredible work you do in mental health awareness. Thank you also to Ian Bishop at Mentemia, for your assistance in this collaboration.

Treena Pitham, 'organiser extraordinaire', cat-herder of heroic proportions and generally all-round-awesome executive assistant. We have been together for so many years now, and every week I feel immensely grateful for your support.

To those leaders who have inspired me and led me in my career, to those people whom I have led in turn and to my clients—ngā mihi nui ki a koutou. I have learnt so much from all of you. Special thanks to Nick Simcock for being a class-act leader back then—and for being a class-act executive coach for me now (every executive coach needs a coach, huh?!). Nick, you da bomb, especially on getting me to do all that financial crap I hate doing but know is important.

To those leadership authors and researchers who have gone before me and whose work and writing inspired and informed me—Christina Maslach and Michael Leiter, Michael Lee Stallard, James Strock, Tanveer Naseer, Brené Brown, and my Twitter friend Ken Downer, to name just a few—I would like to express my gratitude. A special mention to Dr Alison Romney Eyring and Jayne Chater for your pearls of wisdom as I wrote this book. And to Fiona Fenwick for being the first of us three gals to publish a book!

Thank you to my friends who have supported me on this book-writing journey—and on life's journey, for that matter. You gave me words of encouragement as I wrote this book, and those little texts, phone calls and messages have kept me going when the going got tough. To Sarah Brown and Carmel Murphy (The Bridesmaids) and to Amy Cunningham—you make me laugh and see the bright side, as well as being there for me in the best possible way during the tough times. To the 'Amigos WAGS', 'Soul Posse', 'Wine Waka' and to all those other friends who don't have weird group names—thank you so much for the love and support.

To my big brothers Andrew and Magoo—gosh, how lucky I am to have you both. I love that you are proud of me for doing this, but also how you keep me grounded and not too big for my boots. To Mum, you've taught me the value of compassion and love. I would like to think that comes through a little in this book.

A special shout-out to my husband, Doug. Where do I start?! Thank you for believing in me and supporting my career, our family and my hare-brained ideas for over twenty years. I feel so unreservedly loved and supported by you. And in the spirit of our ongoing joke: 'I'm so lucky, but let's not forget—not as lucky as you, babe.'

To my three children, Sienna, Zach and Nicholas; you are the centre of my daisy. Sienna, I love you to the moon and back and infinity plus one, so there. To Zach, 'chur', I hope you think this book is 'hard'—I'm so proud of you, my boy. To Nicholas, thank you so much for forgiving me for leaving you on the footpath all those years ago and for letting me tell our story. I think you turned out more than AOK despite it!

Finally, thank you, Dad, for inspiring me so much when you were alive, and continuing to do so all the way through writing this book.

ABOUT THE AUTHOR

Suzi McAlpine is an international speaker, author of award-winning blog *The Leader's Digest,* and creator of The Leader's Map, an online blended leadership programme for organisations wanting to better equip their emerging leaders. As a leadership development specialist, Suzi writes and speaks about accomplished leadership, what magic emerges when it's present, and how to ignite better leadership in individuals, teams and organisations.

Her other area of passion relates to recognising and addressing burnout in organisations, following her own experience and the front-row seat she's had in her role as an executive coach. With a BBS in Management (first-class honours), Suzi's career has spanned a variety of industries and positions, culminating in her leading the New Zealand practice of a division of the world's largest HR consultancy and executive search firm, before moving into the executive coaching world.

Having been a leader and senior executive herself, Suzi has worked alongside CEOs and executive teams in many guises. Now Suzi is passionate about helping leaders to create environments in which people, as well as profits, thrive.

Suzi is married with three children and lives in Nelson, New Zealand.

PRAISE FOR BEYOND BURNOUT

'The timing of this book is impeccable. It's just what is required in what are unique and challenging times. It raised the burnout radar for me and not only is it likely that I am burnt out but also my team. A great shot in the arm with practical and helpful solutions.'

—Stephen Smith, Chief Executive Officer, MOA Brewing Company

'A wonderful read full of insight and wisdom. The penny dropped for me several times. Suzi has done a masterful job weaving personal stories into fact-based research, giving us solutions that are needed now more than ever. Highly recommended.'

—Shane Anselmi, CEO & Founder Overland Footwear Group, Multi Winners of the IBM Best Workplace NZ Award

'This book is hugely enlightening and a must-read for any people leader in today's world. It is not just what we say as leaders but what we do, and understanding how to help our people thrive in the world we are in, (I would suggest) is the most important part of a leader's role. Whether you are or have experienced burnout or are a leader of people in our changing world, this resource is a must.'

—Jayne Chater, author of *A Slight Detour—A Guide to Successfully Navigating Career and Family,* founder of Reconnect

'*Beyond Burnout* is right on target, a guide that many people today need to help combat the epidemic of job burnout. With actionable insights from the most current research and the author's experience, every leader should race to get his or her hands on it.'

—Michael Lee Stallard, President, Connection Culture Group, author of *Connection Culture* and *Fired Up or Burned Out*

'In our hyper-connected, 24-7, digitised world, there are spectacular new opportunities for leadership and performance excellence. There are also new snares that lay in wait for even the most dedicated and talented. Suzi McAlpine has brilliantly analyzed the latest iteration of the shape-shifting, protean spectre of burnout. Her actionable, relatable insights can make the difference in deciding individual and organizational success or disappointment.'

—James Strock, award-winning author of *Serve to Lead 2.0: 21st Century Leaders Manual,* speaker, entrepreneur, lawyer and former US senior-level public official

'One of the most important things I ever did in my life was work out the "foundations" for my physical and mental health. Sadly I didn't do that until I was in my late 40s. Working it out for myself earlier would have been beneficial to everyone around me, family, friends and the people that reported to me.

It's great to have more conversations and resources like this book to help spark change. There isn't a board meeting I have sat in during the Covid crisis where the "burnout factor" for the CEO and team has not been an issue. I hope that has been the case across the world.'

—Jana Rangooni, Media Industry Executive and Independent Director.

'Not many business-oriented books see me welling up with a tear. Suzi's book on burnout did! Suzi goes into a detailed, data-based analysis of burnout—how to identify it, what to do about it and the enormous costs it carries. Upon reading it I realised that my badge of pride at "slacking" my other directors regularly at 1am, along with my other behaviours, were signalling burnout. There is some leadership gold here, along with a trove of useful and relatable tools. Highly recommended for anyone grappling with overload in the modern organisation.'

—Josh Comrie, Entrepreneur, Investor, Director.

'This book is a must-read for leaders, with great advice from one of the best leadership coaches I know ... Suzi's pragmatism and vulnerability shine through in every page.'

—Tania Palmer, Chief People Officer, Meridian Energy

'*Beyond Burnout* offers a timely prescription on how to address the growing issue of burnout in today's workplaces. A must-read for leaders looking to not only better understand what causes burnout, but what they can do to help employees suffering from burnout to once again succeed and thrive.'

—Tanveer Naseer, MSc., Inc. 100 leadership speaker, award-winning leadership writer, and author of *Leadership Vertigo*.

Index

A
absenteeism, *15, 16, 17*
accomplishment, sense of, *173, 175, 177*
age differences, *76*
Australia, *106, 222, 224*
   see also Cogo Workplace Wellbeing Survey,

B
burnout,
   causes, *64, 65, 95, 96, 97, 99, 100, 103, 105, 106, 108, 110, 112, 114, 116, 117, 119, 121, 122, 125, 126, 128, 130, 131*
   costs, *13, 15, 16, 17, 135*
   definitions, *51, 53, 54*
   extent, *2, 4, 6, 8, 9, 11, 13*
   myths about, *19, 21, 22, 26, 28, 30, 32, 33, 35, 36, 38, 40, 42, 43, 45*

C
China, *106*
Cogo Workplace Wellbeing Survey, *6, 8, 9, 11, 33, 40, 42, 68, 70, 72, 74, 83, 85, 87, 90, 103, 119, 122, 126, 133, 137, 186, 193, 200, 208, 228, 229, 240, 244*
counselling services, *133, 202, 204, 206, 301*
   see also support programmes,
Covid-19, *11, 225, 237*
cynicism towards workplace, *8, 9, 53, 64, 74, 156, 165, 167, 169, 170, 171*

D
depression, *53, 58, 60, 62, 64, 65, 195, 208, 222*

E
emergency service workers, *80*

emotional intelligence, *251*
Employee Assistance Programme (EAP), *133, 202, 301, 334*
executives (senior), *87, 88, 90, 92*
exercise (physical), *311, 313*
exhaustion, *6, 16, 40, 42, 51, 103, 121, 160, 161, 163, 164*

G
gender and burnout, *70, 72, 74, 76*

H
high performers, *30, 32*

I
isolation,
   see social isolation,

J
Japan, *106*

L
leadership, *139, 140, 142, 144, 146, 147, 148, 181, 182, 188, 190, 196, 198, 200, 202, 204, 206, 208, 210, 212, 213, 232, 244, 245, 247, 249, 251, 281, 283, 285, 286, 288*
   coaching and, *19, 21, 241*
   delegation, *281, 283, 288, 290, 292*
   of vulnerable staff, *323, 325, 326, 329, 330, 332, 334, 335*
legal profession, *83, 258*
Leiter, Michael, *64, 65, 95, 97, 128, 150*
LGBTQ susceptibility, *76*
long hours, *42, 54, 81, 83, 99, 100, 105, 106, 108, 277, 288*
   see also overwork,

M
male burnout, *70, 72, 74*

Maslach, Christina, *26, 97, 128*
medical profession, *6, 81, 103*
meditation, *313*
mental health, *198, 200, 202, 204, 206, 208, 210, 212, 213, 215, 217, 218*

N
New Zealand, *81, 106, 222*
   see also Cogo Workplace Wellbeing Survey,

O
one-on-one meetings, *182, 210, 255, 281, 334*
organisational practices, *146, 147, 182, 184, 232, 233, 235, 237, 239, 240, 241, 258, 259, 261, 263, 264, 267, 268, 270, 271, 273, 275, 277, 279, 281*
overwork, *30, 32, 99, 100, 103, 105, 106, 108, 110, 258, 259, 261, 263, 264, 267, 268, 270, 277, 279*
   see also long hours,

P
personality traits, *76, 78*
professions, differences among, *80, 81, 83, 85, 87*

R
recognising signs,
   see signs of burnout,
reward, sufficiency of, *116, 117*

S
shame over burnout, *190, 191, 193, 195, 196*
shift work, *43*
signs of burnout, *6, 8, 142, 144, 150, 152, 154, 156, 157, 159, 160, 161, 163, 164, 165, 167, 169, 170, 171, 173, 175, 177, 179, 181, 182, 184*
social isolation, *8, 16, 40, 42, 43, 87, 103, 117, 119, 121, 122, 125, 146, 220, 222,*

224, 225, 228, 229, 232, 233, 235, 237, 239, 240, 241, 244, 245, 247, 249, 251, 253, 255
South Korea, *106*
stigma and destigmatising, *144, 146, 186, 188, 190, 191, 193, 195, 196, 198, 200, 202, 204, 206, 208, 210, 212, 213, 215, 217, 218*
stress, *38, 40, 42, 51, 53, 54, 56, 57, 58, 60, 62, 64, 137*
   contributing factors, *72, 74*
support programmes, *9, 133, 137, 334*
   see also counselling services,

T
teaching profession, *83, 85*
technology, *110, 225, 235, 237, 239, 316*
time management, *290, 315, 316*
time off, *35, 36, 311, 334*

U
United Kingdom, *28, 135, 224*
United States, *4, 6, 9, 11, 16, 35, 43, 106, 119, 222, 224*

V
values conflicts, *128, 130, 131*

W
Wheel of Life, *309*
women and burnout, *70, 72, 74, 76*
Workplace Wellbeing Survey,
   see Cogo Workplace Wellbeing Survey,
World Health Organization, *17, 51, 53, 193*

CPSIA information can be obtained
at www.ICGtesting.com
Printed in the USA
LVHW090735170223
739598LV00035B/2119